# A Recovery Strategy

# for Europe

# Federal Trust Report

# THE FEDERAL TRUST

The Federal Trust for Education and Research was founded in 1945 to be the research arm of Federal Union. The aim of the Trust is to study the theory and practice of federal government. The principal focus of its work has been the European Community and the United Kingdom's place within it.

The Trust conducts inquiries, promotes seminars and conferences and publishes on a wide range of contemporary issues. Its future work programme includes continuing study of Economic and Monetary Union, a major enquiry into the role of national parliaments within the EC and an exercise in building alternative scenarios for Europe's future. A book on the implications of the Treaty of Maastricht will be published in Spring 1994. The longer term objective of the Trust is to contribute towards a constitutional settlement for the New Europe.

The Trust also sustains a major programme of European civic education for sixth forms, universities and young leaders.

The Federal Trust, which is chaired by John Pinder, is the UK member of TEPSA (the Trans-European Policy Association).

# A Recovery Strategy for Europe

## A Federal Trust Report

Edited by Harry Cowie & John Pinder

Published by the Federal Trust
158 Buckingham Palace Road
London SW1W 9TR
Telephone 071-259 9990
Fax 071-259 9505

© Federal Trust for Education and Research 1993

ISBN No. 90157344-2

The Federal Trust is a registered charity

Cover photograph © Eurotunnel

Produced by PSI Publishing, London NW1 3SR

Printed in Great Britain by BPCC Wheaton's, Exeter

# CONTENTS

# Acknowledgements

The British contribution to the debate about the future of the European Community has not, in recent years, been influential. Those who write for the Federal Trust are motivated by the wish to make the EC work better. This short book was invoked by the Delors initiative of June 1993 to stimulate debate about economic recovery. The authors share many of the Commission's views about the nature of the European crisis, and offer here their individual assessments and prescriptions. The Trust is most grateful to the authors for their prompt and imaginative contributions, and to Harry Cowie and John Pinder for taking editorial responsibility.

Guillaume McLaughlin, the Trust's publications officer, and Nick Evans of PSI have also been vital to the production of this book.

The Federal Trust welcomes readers' reactions to its reports.


**Andrew Duff**
Director

London
5 November 1993

# About the Authors

**Harry Cowie** is currently Senior Research Fellow at the Federal Trust. Formerly a research director for the Liberal Party, he has worked as an economic consultant and a London stockbroker.

**Graham Bishop** has been Vice-President of Salomon Brothers International since 1983. He has previously worked in the City of London as an international economist and pension fund manager.

**Yao-Su Hu** is Principal of the Hong Kong Shue Yan College. He has been a Professor at Warwick University and visiting professor at the Administrative Staff College.

**Christopher Wilkinson** is Head of the International Technological Unit, DG XIII, of the EC Commission. He worked at the IBRD and OECD before joining the Commission in 1973.

**Ian Mackintosh** is Director of the European Foundation for Technical Innovation and visiting professor at University College, London. He was previously Executive Chairman of an IT Consultancy and an R&D Director of Westinghouse Laboratories.

**Keith Richardson** is Director-General of the European Round Table of Industrialists. He was previously industrial editor of the Sunday Times.

**Andrew Warren** has been Founder-Director of the Association for the Conservation of Energy since 1981. In 1993 he was appointed as a special advisor to the House of Commons Environment Committee.

**David Goodhart** is currently labour editor at the Financial Times having formerly been the Bonn correspondent. He has published many books and articles on employment issues.

**Frank Field** is chairman of the Commons Select Committee on Social Security having been Labour MP for Birkenhead since 1979. He is the former director of the Child Poverty Action Group and the Low Pay Unit.

**Jonathan Hoffman** has been Director of Economics at Credit Suisse First Boston since 1989. He has previously worked at the Bank of England.

**John Pinder** is Chairman of the Federal Trust and a visiting professor at the College of Europe, Bruges. He was Director of the Policy Studies Institute from 1964 to 1985.

# Chapter One

# Driving Forces Towards Recovery

## Harry Cowie

The scale and character of Europe's unemployment problem currently dominates the agenda of the European Community (EC). Action is needed if the problem is not seriously to impair the Community's competitiveness and inflict considerable damage to the social fabric of the member states. The debate has begun. The European Council at Copenhagen in June 1993 asked the Commission to prepare a White Paper on a strategy for the economic renewal of the Community. At that meeting President Delors, after analysing the strengths and weaknesses of the European economy, presented his "guidelines for economic renewal in Europe".[1]

Delors cited six weaknesses of the European Community. First and foremost came the high rate of unemployment. He pointed out that between 1970 and 1990, the United States created 28.8 million jobs, Japan 11.7 million and the European Community only 8.8 million. Within the Community, 16 unemployed out of every hundred are under 25 years of age and one unemployed person out of five under 25 had (in 1991) been looking for work for two years. Secondly, the Community's competitiveness had fallen over the past two years. Its share of world markets had fallen by 3.7% in comparison with 1980, while that in the United States increased by 2.2% and in Japan by 0.5%. Thirdly, the attempts by the EC to increase internal cohesion between rich and poor countries had been complicated by the changing international division of labour, in particular the industrial relocation towards Pacific Rim countries with low wage costs and rising productivity through rapid adoption of high technology. Fourthly, there are fears that the existing wave of new technology, at least in the short term, may destroy employment — in contrast to previous waves based on the development of energy and car industries.

Fifthly, job creation on the scale necessary to get unemployment down from the current levels to more acceptable levels — say 5% — cannot be achieved on the basis of even the relatively high levels of the second half of the 1980s which achieved 3.5% economic growth and 2% productivity growth. The Community will have to create extra jobs on a scale large enough, not only to absorb the currently recorded unemployed, but also meet the demands of those who will enter the labour market.

Sixthly, as levels of employment depend not only on the rate of economic growth, but on the employment-intensity of that growth, the Community must direct its attention to labour market policies. Less than 60% of the Community's population of working age are in work compared with over 70% in Scandinavia where there are high activity rates among women.

## Flexible labour

There is little doubt that as the Tokyo G7 Summit concluded "reducing unemployment ... requires structural reforms to improve the efficiency of markets, particularly labour markets". The US job creation record over the past two decades of more than 28 million extra jobs compared with under 9 million in the Community is often cited as a classic illustration of the virtues of flexible labour. Nevertheless, the US is the only leading industrialised country where many low-income workers have experienced substantial real pay cuts. Real hourly wages of men with 12 or fewer hours of schooling fell about 20% between 1979 and 1989 when comparable UK workers experienced 12% increased earnings. Indeed it has been suggested that the US created far more jobs than any other industrial economy, "largely because of unusually intense demographic pressures: the arrival in the workforce of the outsized 'baby boom' generation, the shift of women into paid employment and substantial immigration — six million people entered the US in the 1980s alone, the largest influx since the early years of the century... For many Europeans, US labour markets will seem an unattractive role model. Stagnant real wages, rising inequality and limited job security will strike many as a high — perhaps unacceptable — price to pay for relatively low jobless rates". [2]

Japan has also succeeded in achieving higher rates of employment than the Community. In particular, Japan has very successfully created an advanced technology sector in competitively traded goods which, as a result of high productivity, has been able to generate real income growth that has in turn created jobs in the service sector. By contrast, productivity in the Japanese service and distribution sector is relatively low, thereby generating more employment — even though earnings in industry and services are much the same in both cases. Many commentators have attributed the Japanese miracle at least in part to a successful partnership between state, finance and industry. Japan's post-war success in planning shifts in industrial dominance from textiles to shipping and then to cars and electronics has been guided by MITI that seemed to have an instinct for protecting the industries of the future while helping sunset industries to leave the scene quietly and with dignity. One commentator has contrasted the behaviour of Western governments who usually do the opposite, caving in to pressure from workers to protect textiles and shipbuilding, in which newly industrialising countries (NICs) are already more competitive, while not doing enough to help infant industries in high-technology and information industries which are not necessarily large employers.[3]

The current recession in Japan has exposed widespread structural problems that have provoked fear that corporate Japan's tradition of jobs for life will break down. So far, Japanese companies have managed to avoid making wide-spread redundancies, and this has helped to keep the unemployment rate at 2.5%. The job market weakness is a symptom of wider change in their economy reflecting the continued shift of manufacturing capacity out of Japan to cheaper locations in South-East Asia.

## Policy options

It is not easy to transfer lessons in job creation from the US or Japan to Europe. Nevertheless, the differences that exist are sufficiently wide to prompt consideration of all possible policy options open to the Community. At the same time it is necessary to identify approaches that are both adaptable to the Community and compatible with its overall economic and social aims. In particular, the EC would need to ensure that any changes to existing policies were carried out in ways that do not exploit workers in a weak position in the labour market, or inhibit the development of the high value-added, knowledge-based jobs which will be the key to future competitiveness.

There are short and medium term causes of the high level of unemployment in the Community which are not included in the catalogue of Jacques Delors summarised at the start of this Chapter. One major cause for the current European recession is the severe economic shock brought about by the absorption of the Eastern Länder into the Community. As Sir Leon Brittan commented: "It was never going to be as easy as it looked at the time and it is fair to say that we under-reacted to the macro-economic impact of unification — a response which has not only deepened recession but has also jeopardised the future of economic and monetary co-operation in Europe". [4]

## Driving forces

There are also long-term driving forces at work in the major industrial societies that are helping to lay the foundations of the 21st century. A Federal Trust study group identified the following driving forces at work in Europe: technological change, financial integration, environmental pressures, social trends, democratic aspirations and interdependence among states. Driving forces interact with political structures and influence their development. The different political structures can accommodate or frustrate the driving forces to differing degrees.[5]

Historians have noted that, periodically, the world brings forth a wave of new technology of such a revolutionary nature that it transforms the whole basis of economic activity. Steam power, electric power and the internal combustion engine are past examples of such "mainstream technologies". Their adoption ultimately affects almost every aspect of lifestyle and profoundly affects changes in production, management and governmental organisations. The first two to three decades of the new wave of technology tends to be accompanied by massive structural change as the older industries of the previous wave are in decline and the new industries can be subject to rapid technological change and price competition. A good example is provided by the mass-production techniques originating in the American automobile industry and rapidly diffusing into many other sectors. Mass production required the evolution of the modern corporation with the development of advertising and marketing techniques to persuade the consumer to buy standardised products. Even before the age of mass production, however, it had already been noted by commentators that Americans were much more willing to all wear the same apparel. 'Keeping-up-with-the-Joneses' was a necessary ingredient in the American equation which permitted Henry Ford to launch a standard black model T Ford on a mass-produced basis while, in marked contrast, the European motor industry (where the fundamental innovations in the development of the internal combustion engine had taken place) was producing for a highly differentiated upper-middle-class market. Finally, the Roosevelt administration, faced with an unprecedented economic crisis in the early 1930s, established the New Deal which laid the basis for the infrastructure of roads and suburban life that could cater for an increasingly motorised society.

**Information technology**

There is little disagreement that information technology (IT) is the mainstream technology of the current era. It took off with the development of the microprocessor in the early 1970s. Around that time growth industries of the previous wave, namely steel, plastics and many other began to demonstrate signs of overcapacity. The next two decades of the 1970s and 1980s witnessed growing structural problems as the advanced nations had to cope with the eradication of excess capacity in the older industries while learning to live with the impact of the new technology. IT has already revolutionised the world of finance and communications. Money is an information product. As Richard O'Brien has pointed out the very essence of money is not so much in its physical appearance as in the information it conveys, whether as a debt, a store of value or a medium of exchange.[6] The economics of financial services are being radically revised as a result of the reductions in costs associated with the new technology. However, full advantage of the economies of scale can only be achieved if the cosy compartmentalisation of both capital markets and financial services is swept away.

In the same way, as digital technology penetrates the worlds of telecommunications, radio and television, publishing and office machinery, so these previously separate activities begin to lose their individual identity and merge. This is the world of cable television, cellular phones, intelligent fax, desk-top publishing and value-added networks. The economics of telecommunications provide an example of the extent to which the new technology has acted as a driving force for a more integrated Europe. National markets are too small to support the necessary R&D or to give the leading companies the framework they need in which to compete with their Japanese and American equivalents. The software cost for a public switching system that incorporates about 3 million programmed instructions represents 80% of the total cost of the system; in 1970 the proportion was 20%. The R&D cost of such a system is now at least Ecu 1 billion, whereas the electro-mechanical systems of 1970 cost only Ecu 15 - 20 million. Investment on this scale cannot be undertaken unless one can count on obtaining 8% of the world market. None of the national markets in the Community amounts to more than 6% whereas Japan has 11% and the United States 35%.[7]

It is, therefore, no longer possible or desirable to develop European telecommunications according to the traditional model of 'national champions' — a strategy which has led to the development of eight different types of digital switching systems in Europe compared with two in Japan and three in the United States.

Information technology has also resulted in radical changes in many manufacturing and distribution sectors. The introduction of flexible manufacturing techniques, robot assembly, just-in-time inventory control, computer-aided design and electronic messaging is bringing about another management revolution comparable to the mass-production era. As a recent report of the EC Commission commented:

> "The demands of world competition mean that it is time to move from the 'Fordist' model of production, with mass production of standardised products, to flexible models which combine economies of scale and of scope where the search for quality and variety in goods means a constant renewal of products. A very well-known

example is that of 'lean production' which in contrast to mass-production, allows major savings in personnel, stocks and time."[8]

## Two fallacies

Among the apparent weaknesses of the European Community, cited by President Delors, there is the fear that the existing wave of new technology destroys jobs in contrast to previous waves based on the development of energy and car industries. Secondly, there is concern that Europe cannot compete with the Pacific Rim countries. In fact each wave of new technology from the application of steam power to textiles has led to concern that permanent unemployment could be the lot of displaced workers. But the fear that Europe will somehow be unable to compete across the board and that a permanent long-term increase in unemployment is therefore inevitable rests on two false assumptions:

- First, there is a single 'lump' of work for competing economies to do. This is clearly false. As developing countries and NICs continue to expand the Community will increasingly specialise in producing and exporting high-value-added tradeable goods.

- Second, because differences in productivity between economies are falling, Europe can no longer benefit from international trade. This too is false. Increased prosperity from multinational trade flows from differences in comparative advantage in the production of different goods and services, and not from absolute differences in productivity levels. Furthermore the Pacific Rim countries do not export to line their central bank vaults with dollars or marks but do so in order to import. Can Europe supply a growing proportion of their needs? In order to do so, the Community will have to be in the vanguard of the IT revolution. Delors has called for the creation of a European information infrastructure to serve as the artery of the new economy and so stimulate the information industry. Ian Mackintosh in Chapter 5 suggests where the EC should concentrate its action in order to build such a Eurogrid.

## Eurogrid and lifestyles

The construction of a Eurogrid or information infrastructure would give a powerful impetus to the development of new needs. So far the impact on the lifestyle of the family has been less than that of the last two waves based on the development of electricity and the car. The microprocessor is not yet as ubiquitous as the small electric motor which powers the multitudes of appliances and gadgets in today's homes and cars.

Nevertheless their number is increasing and they are already found in such items as video recorders, CD players, watches, calculators, central heating controllers and washing machines. New generation products such as intelligent telephones and home fax machines are already common. France's Minitel and the UK's Teletext represent early experiments in home-orientated information systems. In-car navigation systems are being researched and prototyped in the USA, Europe and Japan. Teleshopping, telebanking and teleworking are still in their infancy.

The Community has to ensure that a growing proportion of the new products are manufactured in Europe. For too long the member countries have tended to try to preserve their national champions when it comes to allocating R & D expenditure. Yet the dynamism of industry is the crucial factor in the success or failure of an innovative policy. The Community can help to strengthen important external factors, such as access to a large and sophisticated market and a solid scientific and technological base including high-quality human resources. Instead of preserving the old companies, a successful strategy would create an industrial fabric which is itself dynamic and which is regularly rejuvenated by the appearance of new companies. The road ahead in industrial policy is outlined by Christopher Wilkinson in Chapter 4.

## Infrastructure networks

President Delors has also called for an efficient network of transport and telecommunications infrastructure. The European Growth Initiative launched at the Edinburgh Council in December 1992 provides for a loan facility of Ecu 5 billion for large-scale infrastructure programmes such as TGV, inland waterways, roads and motorways. As Keith Richardson outlines in Chapter 6 there is a great need for a pan-European network of improved transport and telecommunications infrastructure to complement the existing motorway and TGV schemes which are based largely on national grids. Delors has called for an ambitious programme of Ecu 30 billion a year to be invested in such schemes which would considerably increase the competitiveness of the European economy by making it easier and cheaper for people, goods and services to move around the Single Market. It would also give a much needed stimulus to the construction and transport industries. Public-private partnerships would provide a useful vehicle for constructing these networks. Funds from an enlarged European Growth Initiative supplemented by loans from the European Investment Fund could be used as leverage to attract a much higher proportion of private capital.

## Environmental pressures

Public concern about the environment has been growing and will continue to do so. It will be an increasingly powerful driving force for European integration in order to achieve sustainable economic development and a better quality of life. Nature is a unique resource, and its depletion and pollution must bear a price. In general, market mechanisms are the most effective way in which to change social behaviour and to create new economic opportunities.

In Chapter 7 Andrew Warren suggests that taking into account the environment will create new jobs. Given the right financial incentives there is certainly a large labour-intensive programme of energy conservation that can be undertaken. The CBI has estimated that the world market for environmental protection and services will grow from £200 billion in 1990 to £300 billion in 2000.[9] At the same time the taxing of scarce natural resources through a carbon/energy tax should make it possible to reduce excessive taxes on labour — with beneficial consequences for Europe's economic competiveness. Member governments could use revenue from the EC tax to promote energy conservation. Sustainability also requires a real change in our approach to waste management.

## Quality of life

The social problems and technological change of the next two decades are likely to be accompanied by changing values. Until recently the pace-makers in society have been 'outer-directed' in their values, concerned with materialistic goals of improved living standards motivated by peer group pressure. Social analysts point to the use of a more 'inner-directed' group since the early 1970s who put a high priority on the quality of life, self-development and individual freedom and responsibility. This class is attracted by the new information technology as it permits them to be more involved in decision-making while being, at the same time, leaner in its use of natural resources. This 'post-materialist' group could be the pace-maker in the pursuit of new attitudes to employment which the Commission has identified, in particular the following:[10]

* adaptability at the workplace, and the potential for developing new forms of employment based on new forms of work organisation;

* the development of new working time structures able to expand employment opportunities;

- the development of new working time structures able to expand employment opportunities;

- the development of training systems and qualifications able both to improve integration into the labour market and to anticipate structural change;

- investigation of the scope for reducing labour costs and increasing employment intensity, notably by modifying the incidence of taxation systems;

- exploitation of the employment growth-potential of new areas of work — the environmental industries, the arts and household services.

## Towards an integrated market

Most European governments would not want to go down the American route of creating a large number of low-wage service sector jobs which have been subject to falling real wages in the last two decades. In any case greater flexibility of labour markets is only part of the explanation of the better job creation record in the USA. The United States is already an integrated economy with a single currency and much greater factor mobility than Europe in terms of both labour and capital. The Single European Market has been a giant stride in the direction of a freer market but considerable obstacles remain before the Community is a truly integrated market.

In the meantime it is increasingly being acknowledged in the EC that the balance has swung too far towards employment protection and away from job creation. David Goodhart analyses the current position in Chapter 8. He points out that national governments are moving in the right direction of tackling the factors underlying the rigidities, although a great deal more requires to be done. One of the most serious obstacles to job creation is the high non-wage labour costs that are incurred in many continental European countries. Pay-roll taxes add on average 30% to EC wage costs and the average figure can be as high as 45% in France, Belgium and Italy, and as low as 3% in Denmark and 13% in the United Kingdom— which finances social security schemes largely through general taxation and where a growing proportion of pensions are paid through privately funded schemes.

## Beyond the Welfare State

Frank Field and Jonathan Hoffman point out in Chapter 9 that state pensions at present represent Europe's Achilles heel. Demographic and financial pressures mean that European governments require larger payroll taxes to fund the growing deficits on state pension schemes. If these pay-as-you-go schemes, that are at present funded on a levy on the existing working population, were replaced with private sector pensions that were invested in funded schemes, there would be an enormous boost to the size of loanable funds available to promote job flexibility between regions and states. Without this growth in private investment, the Single Market will not be fulfilled.

At present the UK, Denmark, the Netherlands and Ireland are the only EC countries where funded pension schemes are fully developed and their combined assets account for 82% of the total pension fund assets in the EC. As a result UK pension funds account for over one-fifth of household assets, nearly ten times the equivalent German proportion. Furthermore a significant share of Europe's life assurance and pension fund assets remain trapped within their domestic borders despite the Single Market. The European Federation for Retirement Provision has warned that a new Directive could attempt to tighten the limits of the proportion of assets which may be invested abroad because many member governments are obliging pension funds to place a high proportion of their investments into their national government bonds. Such blatant national self-interest would be counter-productive. Every 1% improvement in pension fund investment returns reduces employers' costs by 2-3% of the payroll. If governments want to tackle unemployment they should allow the pension funds to maximise their returns.

### Keystone in the arch

The keystone in the arch is the provision of a single currency. There is likely to be considerable resistance to the freedom to move pension fund and life assurance investment throughout the EC as long as there is fear of currency devaluation. Yet, as Graham Bishop emphasises in Chapter 2, the freedom of capital movements that exists at present already means that marginal movements of assets on a precautionary basis — say 3% of UK's institutional assets — can absorb all of the country's foreign exchange reserves, as indeed happened on 'Black Wednesday'. The draw of the largest and most liquid capital market in the world could be very considerable, acting as a powerful magnet to investors from the US and Japan. Even if the Ecu 1500 billion already in Europe's life assurance and pension funds were efficiently allocated the stimulus to growth could be considerable. A switch to funded schemes from the existing pay-as-you-go basis points to a pool of financial assets in excess of Ecu 6000 billion in the foreseeable future. Finally, the creation of a more integrated European capital market could be a major step towards reducing the cost of capital and the means of funding the infrastructure schemes outlined in this report. [11]

## Political will

The final and possibly most important ingredient in a European recovery package is political will. The long drawn out process of negotiating, ratifying, qualifying and now implementing the Treaty on European Union seems to have left the Community adrift. There has been an unfortunate tendency to let the economic stagnation of the early 1990s spill over into the political field. Few political leaders have acknowledged that the way to combat public disillusion and bewilderment in 'Europe' is to improve systematically the quality of the Community's contribution to economic recovery. Too many political leaders have gone on the defensive and have tended to take refuge in diluting the force of the Maastricht Treaty or, worse, in dissembling about its political characteristics and potential force and value. Against this background, the recovery initiative of Jacques Delors is especially welcome.

Now almost 20 million of the EC's total population of 340 million are out of work. In 1993 EC industrial investment will fall by 9% in volume terms. This means that a big, concerted effort to stimulate demand in the European economy is required. The extra public borrowing needed to allow governments to contribute towards this new investment will add less to public deficits than the long-term cost of continuing recession. But EC member governments have failed to act much beyond the level of rhetoric. At the time of writing, the GATT negotiations look some distance from reaching a successful conclusion. The 'growth initiative' of a total of Ecu 7 billion agreed at the December 1992 Edinburgh European Council is badly underspent. EC spending on R&D remains at only 4% of the total EC budget. In 1993, in its bid to restrict domestic spending, the UK Conservative government has refused to allow local government to take up over £300 million of available EC regional development grants. The only big, new investment in British infrastructure (with help from the EIB) is the Jubilee Line extension to Docklands: the modern rail link from Heathrow airport to central London remains a fiction; the English end of the Channel Tunnel railway will mock this generation of politicians. It is small wonder that Britain has declined to become the EC's fifth poorest state, or that crime in our cities has hit unprecedented and seemingly uncontrollable dimensions.

11

In Europe's bid to break the economic cycle of debt and inflation, EMU offers real hope. The recent disruption to the ERM affects EMU only in so far as it changes political attitudes to the Maastricht project. It was always going to be difficult to manage a fixed exchange rate system on the basis of independent monetary policies. As Leon Brittan has argued, regular currency realignments within the EMS could, and no doubt should have taken place. At the end of this decade it is still probable that a significant core group of EC states will conform to the Maastricht criteria and will be prepared to exercise the political will to go forward to a common currency. That vital decision will be made easier, and its consequences more popular, if real economic recovery has taken shape and the EC is seen to have been part of the solution to Europe's economic malaise rather than part of the problem. Long-term investment, continuing liberalisation and deepening integration are the answer.

[1] Agence Europe, 21/22 June 1993.
[2] Michael Prowse, 'No easy answer to job questions', *Financial Times*, 21 July 1993.
[3] Dick Wilson, *The Sun at Noon*, London: Hamish Hamilton, 1986.
[4] Sir Leon Brittan QC *The Future of the European Economy*, Lecture to CEPR, London, 24 September 1993.
[5] The Federal Trust, *Europe's Future: Four Scenarios*, London, 1991.
[6] Richard O'Brien, *Global Financial Integration: The End of Geography*, London: RIIA, 1992.
[7] Eurofile, *Telecommunications, the new highways for the Single European Market*, EC Commission, October 1988.
[8] EC Bulletin Supplement, 2/92 *Research After Maastricht, Brussels, 1992*.
[9] Cited in the House of Lords EC Select Committee, *Industry and the Environment* 18th Report 1992-93.
[10] EC Commission, *Community-wide Framework for Employment*, 16 May 1993.
[11] The Federal Trust, *Towards an Integrated European Capital Market*, Rapporteur Dick Taverne QC, London, 1993.
[12] Conclusions of the Presidency, Copenhagen 21-22 June 1993.

**Appendix to Chapter One**

**Entering the 21st Century**

Eight guidelines for economic renewal in Europe presented by
President Delors to the Copenhagen European Council,
21-22 June 1993, and adopted by it.[12]

## 1. Staying on course for Economic and Monetary Union

A single currency would:

- consolidate the single market and create the necessary conditions for fair and productive competition;

- make investment more attractive, both in the Community and outside, and generally stimulate saving to provide the necessary funds for major infrastructure projects;

- have a stabilizing effect on the international monetary system and discourage the speculation responsible for so much instability and uncertainty.

In order to achieve this, we must:

- get back on the road to convergence, which will boost growth and create jobs throughout the Community — a positive sum game;

- provide national policies and business strategies with a credible, clear and comprehensible perspective and to this end, make the single market productive;

- strengthen the link between European integration and the aspirations of ordinary people by pointing out the benefits to be gained from developing the Community and extending those benefits to other European countries, particularly those in Eastern and Central Europe, with their enormous potential for growth, which would benefit us all.

## 2. The Community as an open and reliable partner in the world

The Community must keep up its efforts to bring the Uruguay Round to a swift conclusion with a balanced agreement covering all the problems now outstanding. The agreement must pave the way for the transition of a world trade organization to reflect the globalisation of markets and business strategies.

This organisation must, without exception, be based on multilateralism, both in spirit and in practice. The way it operates must be determined by other economic realities such as currency movements, capital flows, the need to share the cost of environmental protection fairly and to deliver the social progress to which everyone has a right by a gradualist approach compatible with economic progress.

## 3. Increased co-operation in the field of R & D

We must:

- aim to devote 3% of GNP to research, development and innovation (as against 2% at present);

- concentrate Community action on what can complement and enhance the policies of member states and businesses; and

- at European level and with the support provided by Community action, create frameworks for co-operation between businesses to help them harness innovation and adapt production processes.

## 4. An efficient network of transport and telecommunications infrastructure

Making it easier and cheaper for people, goods and services to move around will increase the competitiveness of the European economy. Efficient infrastructure neworks will be of inestimable value for regional planning and economic and social cohesion.

We must give ourselves ten years in which to stimulate the European industries involved in designing and building these networks (transport, construction, public works, etc.) An overall total of Ecu 30 billion a year seems to be a realistic minimum target for expenditure in this field.

## 5. Common information area: the new technological revolution

We must aim for a decentralised economy, with a properly trained workforce and an abundance of small and medium-sized businesses all co-operating with one another. To achieve this, we need to create a "European information infrastructure" to serve as the real arteries of the economy of the future and to stimulate the information industry (i.e. telecommunications, computers, fibre optics, etc.) with the prospect of abundant supply over a number of years. An initial investment of ECU 5 billion is required, followed by a ECU 5-8 billion a year programme.

We must also set up European training courses for these new trades and professions and encourage distance working by computer (not only for people in the data-processing industry itself but also for those working in education, medicine, social services, environmental protection, urban planning ... and those involved in combating modern-day scourges such as disease, drug abuse and crime).

## 6. Profound changes in our education systems

The priorities here are:

- learning how to keep on learning throughout our lives; combining knowledge with know-how;

- developing each individual's creativity and initiative;

- establishing the right of each individual to lifelong training (all young people would be given vouchers entitling them to initial education and/or training later on).

## 7. Towards a new model of development — taking into account the environment will create new jobs.

Taxing scarce natural resources will make it possible to reduce excessive taxes on labour, thus enhancing Europe's economic competitiveness. Increases in productivity must be used to improve the quality of life and create new jobs; this is the dynamic view of work-sharing: increasing the number of jobs available to cover new qualitative demands, which provide a large range of still unexplored, if not unknown, possibilities.

## 8. More active policies towards the labour market.

Priority must be given to providing everyone on the labour market with a job, activity or useful training. Rather than trying to hold back technological and economic change, we must anticipate it and deal with it in good time.

The quality and the number of job agencies and similar bodies must be increased so as to provide effective help to every person out of work (expenditure needs to rise from 0.1% of Community GDP to 0.5%).

Chapter Two

# Staying on Course for Economic and Monetary Union

## Graham Bishop

The vision of monetary union is rooted in the Treaty of Rome of 1957, but it was powerfully reiterated by the Single European Act in 1985, which also laid the ground for the '1992 programme' to create the Single European Market. The Act enshrined the familiar 'four freedoms': the free movement of goods, persons, services and capital. The Single Market has proved an attractive goal and already has acted as a magnet for many other countries.

Today, the European Community dominates Western Europe and the European Free Trade Association (EFTA) is on the periphery. The EC/EFTA Accord, agreed in November 1991, made the direction quite clear: most of the EFTA states would join the EC in the foreseeable future and, at Maastricht, the European Council effectively invited EFTA states to apply for EC membership. Most have done so. Several will accept the EC's terms and become members — possibly even in January 1995, forming EC-15 (or perhaps EC-16).

Tomorrow, by the year 2000, Europe will be even more dominated by the EC-15. Leaving aside the associates to the East, the population of EC-15 will be as big as the US and Japan combined. Rearranging current GNP figures, the GNP of that group is already a quarter bigger than that of the US. The enlargement process will certainly stretch the EC's institutional structure to its limit and it is clear that another Intergovernmental Conference (IGC) will be necessary in the mid 1990s to consider how to cope with any subsequent expansion. A 1996 IGC has already been specified by the Maastricht Treaty to review foreign and security policy, among other things.

EC-15 would be an economic colossus and it would crystallise if the EC does little more than continue along the current path, following the signposts created in the Treaty of Maastricht. This grouping is planned to have one currency — the Ecu. If this vision turns out to have any truth at all, then the Ecu will rival the dollar tomorrow and surpass it the day after tomorrow. That single currency will be the monetary 'base' for weaving the political tapestry which will result from the present political format — a change so intense that it amounts to a revolution.

## The transition from here to there

That ultimate vision will not crystallise of its own accord. It must be painstakingly built up — starting with today's realities. The first reality is the Single Market and the second is that the Treaty of Maastricht has now ensured that some form of monetary union will occur, associated with the progressive realisation of an integrated capital market. It is this market which will finance the political developments inspired by the spirit of self-determination which is emerging as a driving force of change, so its growth — based on sound money — will provide the backdrop for the Community's political and economic developments in the years ahead.

Simultaneously — but separately — another strand of the argument is being woven: the consumers of Western Europe are growing richer and older and their needs will also be a driving force for change. The eventual strain on social security systems is already apparent to governments and the response is to encourage greater personal saving for retirement. This dovetails with the public's growing wish to hold incremental wealth in the form of financial assets, rather than physical assets.

The entire financial services industry — banks, life insurance, pension funds and mutual funds — is well aware of the consequent growth opportunities. However, it must cope with a variety of regulatory systems intended to protect unsophisticated savers but developed in an era of exchange controls and large government deficits. Achieving the relevant goals of the single market — free movement of capital and services — necessitates a complete review of the regulations which have compartmentalised financial services.

The impact of information technology has outdated many of these compartments and is a force driving the market to evolve towards straightforward competition between various savings products. Having attracted these savings, the institutions must search out profitable ways of deploying their assets because return on capital will be their most powerful sales tool. No type of institution is willing to see its profit opportunities limited by outdated regulations so there is intense pressure for a level playing field. This is the market-driven rationale for a Single Market in money and financial services.

Monetary integration, with its logical culmination in economic and monetary union, supports and extends these market trends. The result is that the combination of a genuinely liberalised and competitive financial services industry, together with the abolition of exchange controls, has brought the drive to EMU close to being a self-perpetuating economic force. But difficulties lie ahead in reconciling this powerful force with deeply rooted political objections.

## The Progress of the Single Market

The EC was founded more than 30 years ago to foster trade between its members. The plan to create a Single Market by 1992 merely took that approach to its logical conclusion. The Single Market has been achieved in broad measure, even without the Maastricht Treaty. Figure 1 sets out the progress of the single financial market, focusing on key directives that will unlock the stock of the Community's long-term savings, and allow them to flow towards higher returns or, more importantly, away from perceived risk. Some measures are already in effect, but all are scheduled to be implemented by mid-1995.

**Figure 1: The Single Financial Market in the EC — Chronology of Events**

| Date Adopted | Directive | Content | DateEffective |
|---|---|---|---|
| 1957 | The Treaty of Rome | "The abolition, as between member states, of obstacles to freedom of movement for persons,servicesandcapital."(Article 3) "member states shall progressively abolish between themselves all restrictions on the movement of capital belonging to persons resident in member states." (Article 67) | |
| 1985 | Directive on Undertakings for Collective Investments in Transferable Securities (UCITS; 85/611/EEC) | "It is desirable that common , basic rules be established for the authorisation supervision, structure,and activities of collective investment undertakings situated in the member states." (Preamble) | 1 Oct 89 |
| 1987 | Single European Act | "The internal market shall comprise an area without internal frontiers in which the free movement of goods, persons, services, and capital is ensured." (Article 8a. Treaty of Rome) | 1 Jan 93 |
| 1988 | Liberalisation of Capital Movements through the Directive for the  capital Implementation of Article 67 (88/361/EEC) | "Member states shall abolish restrictions on movements of taking place between persons resident in member states." (Article1) | 1Jul 90 Greece, Ireland & Portugal 31 Dec 92 |
| 1988 | Second Nonlife Insurance Directive (88/357/EEC) | Insurance of "large risks" anywhere in the EC under home country control. | |

| Date Adopted | Directive | Contents | Date Effective |
|---|---|---|---|
| 1989 | Solvency Ratio Directive (89/647/EEC) | Adopts the Basle Agreement's 0%-100% risk-weightings for credit institutions' assets. Credit institutions to have capital equal to 8% of their risk-weighted assets. | 1 Jan 91 <br><br><br><br> 1 Jan 93 |
| 1989 | Own Funds Directive (89/299/EEC) | Adopts the Basle Agreement's definition of Tier I and Tier II capital for the own funds of credit institutions. | 1 Jan 93 |
| 1989 | Second Banking Directive (89/646/EEC) | ". . . Making possible the granting of a single licence recognised throughout the Community and the application of the principle of home Member State prudential supervision" (Preamble) — the "single passport" concept. | 1 Jan 93 |
| 1990 | Second Life Insurance Directive (90/619/EEC) | Cross-border provision,at policyholder's initiative, of insurance under home country supervision. | 21 May 93 |
| 1991 | Maastricht Agreement on European Union | | 1 Nov 93 |
| 1992 | Third Nonlife Insurance Directive (92/49/EEC) | Single passport for nonlife insurance companies with home-country supervision and EC-wide investment of assets, and a single market for policy-holders. | 1 Jul 94 |
| 1993 | Investment Services Directive firms. | Single passport for securities | |
| 1993 | Capital Adequacy Directive | Capital requirements for securities houses and credit institutions' trading books. | |
| **Subject to Agreement** | | | |
| 1993? | Pension Fund Directive | Cross-border management of funds and EC-wide investment of assets. | |
| Memorandum | | | |
| | | European Monetary Institute to be set up and Stage Two of EMU begins Report on EMU. Stage Three of EMU starts for convergent countries. | 1 Jan 94 <br> By Dec 96 <br><br> By 1 Jan 96 |

## The Single Market and the ERM

Huge capital outflows have depleted the foreign exchange reserves of several EC members and forced these countries to devalue their respective currencies since September 1992. In a fully functional Single Market, will such high outflows be either possible or likely? In addition, what policy responses would be appropriate in this situation, given the liberalising concepts built into the Community at its foundation?

The recent turbulence within the Exchange Rate Mechanism illustrates that foreign exchange reserves are little more than window-dressing: they are wholly inadequate to offset major shifts in a member state's capital stock. This will be even more true in the future as three factors combine and compound: the rise in trade flows and the stock of financial assets; the better management of assets via financial innovation and market efficiency; and the greater liberalisation of financial flows under the Single Market. At present, the classic methods of increasing reserves — devaluation or higher interest rates — are inhibited by ERM rules and the fear of worsening the recession. The formal ERM rules were drastically weakened in August 1993, when the bands were widened to 15%, but most members continue to resist utilising that flexibility fully.

## Rising trade flows

The first stage of the EC's development was to create a customs union to facilitate the trade in goods between member states. This objective has already been attained: in 1958, trade between the 12 countries of the current EC accounted for 6% of their combined GNP; by 1990, this figure had risen to 14%, while GNP had nearly tripled in real terms. However, this increase in trade comes at a price: changes in the lead/lag structure of the mass of payments for this trade can create very large capital flows. In the days of exchange controls, the principal purpose of foreign exchange reserves was to buffer these flows, since the stock of capital was forbidden to move.

Most EC member states have boosted their foreign exchange reserves over the past two decades, often by a factor of five to ten times. However, foreign trade over this period generally has increased at an even faster pace, and the purpose of the Single Market is to allow it to rise even more dramatically in the decades ahead. Thus, the EC authorities' ability to moderate swings in the lead/lag payment structure has been reduced substantially, and will likely decline even further. Figure 2 shows the ratio of one day's trade payments for each EC country relative to its reserves. Typically, reserve coverage has sunk sharply. For example, a one-day adverse swing in France's current trade payments would absorb almost 6% of its reserves versus 3% in 1972.

**Figure 2: European Community — Total Reserves, and Daily Trade Flows as a % of Total Reserves, 1972-Jun 92 (US Dollars in Billions)**

| | Total Reserves Minus Gold | | | Daily Trade Flows as % ofTotal Reserves | | |
|---|---|---|---|---|---|---|
| | 1972 | 1982 | Jun 92 | 1972 | 1982 | Jun 92 |
| Belgium | US$2.2 | US$3.9 | US$14.6 | 4.4% | 9.7% | 6.7% |
| Denmark | 0.8 | 2.3 | 7.1 | 4.7 | 5.7 | 4.1 |
| France | 6.2 | 16.5 | 33.5 | 3.3 | 4.8 | 5.7 |
| Germany | 19.3 | 44.8 | 64.1 | 1.7 | 2.7 | 5.2 |
| Greece | 0.9 | 0.9 | 4.5 | 2.0 | 6.1 | — |
| Ireland | 1.1 | 2.6 | 5.7 | 1.3 | 2.6 | 3.0% |
| Italy | 3.0 | 14.1 | 34.8 | 5.0 | 4.4 | 3.8 |
| Netherlands | 2.7 | 10.1 | 17.7 | 4.5 | 4.6 | 5.4 |
| Portugal | 1.3 | 0.5 | 25.3 | 1.0 | 11.7 | 0.7% |
| Spain | 4.5 | 7.7 | 72.1 | 0.9 | 2.7 | 0.9 |
| UK | 4.9 | 12.4 | 42.6 | 4.0 | 6.1 | 3.6 |

Source: International Monetary Fund.

The EC's success in stimulating trade can be gauged from the inverse order of reserve coverage. Spain and Portugal, the EC's newest members, are most heavily reserved. Ireland, the UK, Italy, and Denmark are in a medium range, while Germany, France, the Netherlands and Belgium/ Luxembourg have the lightest reserve coverage. This last group consists of five of the six founding members of the EC and, therefore, has had the longest experience of rising intra-group trade, and also represents the former core of the ERM.

Foreign trade encompasses factories, stocks, receivables and payables. Companies can easily and immediately calculate their precise foreign exchange exposure. Financial innovation offers the ability to hedge that exposure immediately via the capital markets, as well as through an array of derivative products. The effects of this action can be substantial: for Belgium, a five-day swing in payments for foreign trade would absorb one third of its foreign exchange reserves, although the timing of the payments would reflect the balance of spot and forward transactions. In addition, a company could hedge its stock of items (such as factories and inventories) by extending the hedge to protect all of its exposures to foreign exchange risks rather than just the trade flows alone.

Potential capital flows from trade dictate that the lightly reserved states must guard against these trade payment swings. If these states wanted to keep their respective exchange rates unchanged and pursue independent and genuinely diverse monetary policies, they would need to ban such hedging transactions. But any attempt to block these potential capital flows would strike at the heart of the Community's fundamental goal: free trade. In practice, the problem was effectively resolved by the creation of the ERM core, because no practical alternative was available. The July 1993 crisis has weakened that core and immediately led to a review of desirability of controls. That review rapidly led to a widespread restatement that effective controls were neither possible nor desirable. However, that leaves unresolved the key problem that free movement of capital — in the spirit of the Single Market — is incompatible with semi-fixed exchange rates. This is the incompatibility which led to the description of the ERM as 'half-baked' several years ago. It is now even more urgent that the political 'cooks' return to their task and finish 'baking' because the scale of mobile capital is set to expand even further in the years ahead.

## Financial assets of the ageing population

Foreign exchange reserves are already small relative to the stock of financial assets within the EC. As the stock of assets rises and becomes fully mobile as the Single Market takes hold, the EC's existing foreign exchange reserves will appear diminutive. Demographic projections show that the population of the EC is growing older. The median age of EC citizens was 34 in 1985, but will be 41 in 2010. Germans will top the league with an average age of 44, followed by the Italians at 43, and the French and British at 40. Governments are already wrestling with the implications of demographic ageing on the public funding of pensions: the UK Government abolished its inflation-proof system and leaders in France issued a white paper on possible solutions; a key component of Italy's current stabilisation package is a sharp reduction in the state pension benefit, similar to the one announced in Greece.

These developments will enhance the build-up of a pool of privately funded financial assets to generate retirement income for Europe's citizens. The levels invested in mutual funds almost doubled from Ecu 329 billion in 1987 to Ecu 653 billion in 1991. The European Federation for Retirement Provision has identified about Ecu 800 billion in current pension assets and expects this to reach about Ecu 2300 billion by the year 2000. If the owners of this capital move their funds abroad, then these flows will be buffered by foreign exchange reserves, which totalled only about Ecu 400 billion for the EC in June 1992.

One of the key questions concerning these funds is the extent to which they will be intermediated by financial institutions rather than be held directly by individuals. Italy has one of the highest savings ratios in the EC at 15.6% versus the average of 13%. Nevertheless, its per capita life insurance premiums are only about Ecu 125, compared with Ecu 600 in Germany, Ecu 800 in France and Ecu 1400 in the UK. There are strong public policy reasons to institutionalise these savings to ensure that they are available at retirement, rather than discovering that they have been consumed, with the pensioner then becoming a charge on the public safety-net — a scenario that defeats the original purpose of an individually funded pension system.

The investment behaviour of the beneficial owners of this capital — the pensioners and soon-to-be-pensioners — may change significantly if institutions simply serve as a passive custodian of these funds or compete for a larger share of the pension fund market. Institutions competing on the basis of the investment returns achieved by active portfolio management are more likely to diversify their portfolios internationally and manage them more vigorously. Although policy makers may be tempted to bias the system towards reliance on individual investors' inertia to shift funds overseas in an attempt to ease short-term pressures on foreign reserves, the long-term impact of lower investment returns will still result in poorer pensioners, higher taxes and/or higher costs for employers.

The UK's programme serves as an example of a highly institutionalised system that has already begun to grapple with long-term pension problems. In 1978, a state earnings-related pension scheme (SERPS) was introduced to supplement the basic state pension. In 1988, owing to the potential costs of the scheme, the government reduced the level of benefits available under SERPS to those nationals retiring after the year 2000 because of the cost of the SERPS, and provided incentives to opt out of the scheme. As a consequence, insurance companies' sales of new pension products doubled in that year. Figure 3 shows the scale of build-up in financial assets in the UK (the value has fluctuated with equity market levels).

**Figure 3: UK Financial Institutions — Assets, 1975-91 (Pounds in Billions)**

|  | 1975 | 1980 | 1987 | 1988 | 1989 | 1990 |
|---|---|---|---|---|---|---|
| Pension Funds | — | £53.9 | £227.6 | £267.5 | £339.0 | £302.7 |
| Insurance Co. | £23.3 | 53.8 | 173.4 | 198.4 | 246.2 | 232.3 |
| Investment Trusts | 5.4 | 8.4 | 19.1 | 19.3 | 23.3 | 19.1 |
| Unit Trusts | 2.3 | 4.6 | 33.0 | 39.6 | 55.8 | 41.6 |
| **Total** | **31.0** | **120.7** | **453.1** | **524.8** | **664.3** | **595.7** |
| As %of GNP | 29.3% | 52.1% | 107.0% | 111.3% | 128.9% | 108.2% |
| Pension Funds & Insurance Co.: Cash Flows | £4.1 | £12.1 | £22.0 | £20.0 | £24.5 | £31.6 |

Source: Central Statistical Office.

Although not an EC member, Switzerland serves as an example of a country that has thoroughly grasped the pension nettle.[1] In 1985, the BVG law was enacted to make occupational pension schemes compulsory. The consequent build-up of institutional assets has been dramatic, advancing from 43% of GNP in 1975 to 66% in 1985, and is expected to reach about 110% by the turn of the century.

The results to date of these policy actions suggest that financial assets under institutional management could top 100% of GNP, once a reasonably mature funded pension system is in place. For the EC, that points to a pool of financial assets in excess of Ecu 6000 billion in the foreseeable future. This would be 15 times the level of the member states' current foreign exchange reserves, while a 7% international diversification by those funds would absorb the entire reserves in the absence of any offsetting flows.

## The need for monetary union

In open EC economies, a mature pension system could hold around 20% of its assets abroad. The process of moving to that level of diversification could be lengthy, but such a capital outflow would either place great strain on foreign reserves or would need to be balanced by other inflows, perhaps from a current account surplus. Once the tradition of investing in foreign assets to protect the real value of pension funds is established, then the risk of a currency devaluation is likely to cause a substantial capital outflow. The UK example is a case in point: at the end of 1990, £33 billion of the £596 billion in UK institutional assets were held in cash, while total reserves minus gold amounted to £18.6 billion. If 3% of these assets were put abroad at a time of crisis, this could easily be funded from investors' cash holdings, yet absorb all of the UK's foreign exchange reserves.

The recipients of these foreign inflows may be more constrained than they realise. Investors diversify to reduce risks, so any change in the perception of risk is likely to trigger a sharper reaction from foreign investors than from domestic ones. The collapse in global equity markets in 1987 is widely attributed to worried investors who repatriated their foreign holdings. Another source of alarm could be the risk of assets becoming trapped abroad by the sudden reimposition of exchange controls. In September 1992, Spain unexpectedly reimposed foreign exchange controls, with the resulting outflow of capital causing a 16% fall in the Spanish equity market and a 9% decline in bond prices in the ensuing two weeks. Foreign exchange reserves may have dwindled in significance relative to potential capital flows, but the reaction to the problem of capital movements will be highly significant. If heavy selling of, for example, French francs for Deutschmarks occurred, then the Bundesbank could, in theory, create unlimited reserves for the French Central Bank. In practice, the resultant scale of Deutschmark creation that might be necessary would pressure

German monetary policy unless both countries were prepared to accept the redenomination of a large portion of France's capital stock into Deutschmarks. That type of effective monetary union could only occur under a complete bilateral political agreement, not as a technical result of the shift in capital stocks.

This analysis of the effects of the Single Market demonstrates the interaction of several driving forces: an ageing population building up a massive stock of retirement savings in the form of liquid, financial assets; an effective liberalisation of markets resulting from the success of the Single Market; and the impact of technology in accelerating communications and enhancing the sophistication of financial markets. The combination of these three forces has already put an end to the 'old' ERM. The 'new' ERM will differ sharply and may be barely worthy of the name unless it is a stepping stone to an early monetary union. The impact of these driving forces will not stop there: they will shape the recovery of the European economy — both politically and industrially.

As the governments  search for a recipe for recovery, they remain confronted with a painful dilemma: if they maintain exceptionally high real interest rates in defence of a parity, then economic activity will be stifled. Alternatively, if they allow a sharp currency depreciation and slash interest rates then the short term benefits may be lost as industrialists worry about the weakness of export markets destabilised by competitive currency adjustments.

Solutions might have been found by technical measures of co-operation between independent central banks — in practice, moving close to a de facto monetary union. However, the key state in any such development insGermany and the October Constitutional Court ruling on the Maastricht Treaty seems to have entrenched the requirement that formal political decisions must be taken. This may have condemned the remnants of the ERM to remain half-baked — and act as a serious drag on Europe's recovery. Therefore, a credible recovery strategy may have to be leavened with sufficient political will to complete the baking.

**Implications for the shape of the recovery**

One of the unresolved questions on monetary union is the control of excessive budget deficits. Some countries regard this as infringing their core sovereignty while others see it as a prerequisite of sound European monetary control. Member states' budgets will in any case remain predominant; it seems that the political will may not exist to permit the EC budget to rise from the present level of well below 2% of GDP to even 5%.

One interesting effect of the liberalisation of capital is that particular regions within the member states may benefit. Where sound projects exist, large sums will be available independently of these states' central governments. Thus regional power may increase, at the expense of national governments, as they will be obliged to pursue more conservative fiscal policies if EMU removes their power to print money — the essence of their perfect creditworthiness. Maintaining credit-worthiness will be crucial because the ability of member states' governments to spend will hinge upon the revenue which taxpayers are willing to provide, and at the margin, fresh borrowing. Once the single currency is operational, major imbalances in the central government finances will be completely apparent. The ultimate discipline of the financial markets on such governments is likely to be harsh.

**Tough rules of the Treaty**

In order to guard against these risks, the Treaty of Maastricht sets out several rules in Article 104c: on public deficits, debt levels and borrowing only for investment. These rules are expected to turn back deep-seated trends within EC states. Therefore the state of the European recovery in the mid-1990s will be dominated by the inability of central governments to extend counter cyclical fiscal actions. Indeed, 'Convergence Programmes' constitute rules that require a trend reduction in fiscal deficits.

**Figure 4: European Community: Revenue, Expenditure and Borrowing, 1963-93 (as a % of GDP)**

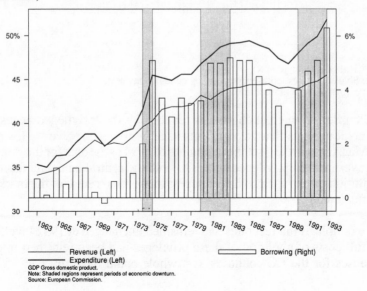

Revenue (Left)
Expenditure (Left)
Borrowing (Right)

GDP Gross domestic product.
Note: Shaded regions represent periods of economic downturn.
Source: European Commission.

## Higher public spending and interest rates

At the first test, the rules-to-be seem to have had little short-run impact on governments. Two years after the 1991 Treaty agreement to limit deficits to 3% of GDP, the aggregate EC deficit has increased to an expected 6% in 1993 — double the proposed limit. Although this increase in borrowing is attributable to the recession to a substantial degree, Figure 1 shows that public expenditure has ratcheted higher for three decades. Increasingly, voter resistance has curtailed tax increases. Europe is likely to face a prolonged and painful adjustment process merely to attain the 3% ceiling. In the meantime, the dead-weight of accumulated deficits will not disappear and the servicing burden has risen sharply in the past decade (see Figure 5). Interest payments will account for 85% of the deficits incurred by EC members in 1993 and will have tripled in the past two decades.

**Figure 5: European Community: Interest Expense (as % of current revenues) and Debt (as % of GDP), 1973-93**

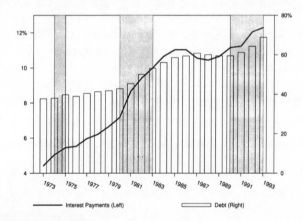

GDP Gross domestic product.
Note: Shaded regions represent periods of economic downturn.
Source: European Commission.

The burden of interest charges is reduced by the 'privileged access' to financial markets that governments usually give themselves. However, the Maastricht Treaty set the beginning of 1994 as the date for the removal of governments' privileged access to both the central bank and financial institutions, although privileged access to the retail sector of the market is unaffected.

For example, if interest rates had remained unchanged at 1992 levels and the full costs of abolition of these privileges had been felt, then interest expenses for the EC countries as a whole could have reached 15% of revenues during 1994. Fortunately, interest rates have declined very sharply, so the upward trend in gearing should be arrested — despite the scale of current deficits. The effects only work through slowly because of the time taken for the government debt portfolio to be refinanced at lower rates as debts mature.

However, the next cyclical up-swing in interest rates could create severe tensions. If debt levels continue to rise relative to GDP, then any failure of political will to curb inflation could lead investors to anticipate inflation and demand a risk premium in interest rates that would start a spiral of rising debt servicing costs. Any such spiral would start from a disturbingly high base for the EC in aggregate — for example, more than a third of the level associated with the UK's decision in the 1930s to take drastic steps to lower the burden of debt servicing.

This growing risk demonstrates the powerful attractions of EMU to the governments of EC members because it is a method of creating a durable climate of price stability to encourage further falls in real interest rates — bringing nominal rates to levels that would eliminate any concerns about debt servicing. Historical precedents suggest that nominal interest rates could fall to 5%, or less, in a world of stable prices.

The debt servicing figures for the EC aggregate disguise a wide dispersion amongst individual states and these are shown in Figure 6. The 1992 data have also been recalculated to show the effect of applying a uniform 5% interest rate to the debt stock.

**Figure 6: Debts and Servicing of EC States, 1992**

|  | Debts % GDP | Interest % of Gov. Revenue 1992 Interest Rates | 5% Int. Rates |
|---|---|---|---|
| Luxembourg | 6.8% | 1.0% | 0.7% |
| France | 50,1 | 6.6 | 5.2 |
| Germany | 45.9 | 7.0 | 4.6 |
| United Kingdom | 45.9 | 8.3 | 6.2 |
| Spain | 47.4 | 10.4 | 5.7 |
| Netherlands | 79.8 | 12.0 | 7.7 |
| Denmark | 74.0 | 12.4 | 6.6 |
| Ireland | 99.0 | 17.9 | 12.2 |
| Portugal | 66.2 | 22.0 | 8.0 |
| Belgium | 132.2 | 24.4 | 14.8 |
| Italy | 106.8 | 25.7 | 11.9 |
| Greece | 105.6 | 38.6 | 14.0 |

Sources: European Commission, Salomon Brothers Inc estimates

The benefits to the highly indebted states are remarkable and underscore the attractions of participating in a durable monetary union that achieves its goal of price stability. The change in the nature of public debt may produce new risks, but great benefits for governments. In the process, national governments will have abided by Community rules and developed appropriate safeguards to ensure that they can be enforced. These rules will be applicable to the public sector as a whole.

While the political cooks search for the elusive recipe for sustained recovery, they will realise that the commitments they made at Maastricht rule out the policy responses used in the last three decades. In any case, the build-up of public debt is becoming dauntingly large and cynical financial markets will readily spot any move towards an inflationary solution to the public debt problem. The magnitude and urgency of the problem could induce the cooks to re-read the recipe they wrote into the cookery book in December 1991 at Maastricht. Ironically, the principal difficulty in using the recipe is that a major ingredient — sound public finance — has been hopelessly scrambled by the cooks themselves.

**Europe of the regions?**

The development of the single Ecu-denominated capital market may have implications for the regions of Europe. The Treaty specifies that public sector borrowings should not exceed investment spending — commonly known as the 'Golden Rule'. The principle of subsidiarity underlies the Political Union component of the Treaty and this may push some political powers to the centre of the EC, but it is quite likely that some will also be pushed down to, or be taken back by the regions. The Ecu capital market of tomorrow will easily be able to finance any worthwhile investment projects, so the regions will then be able to tap a vast pool of savings through this market mechanism, rather than relying on the existing national pool of savings, which are redistributed by taxation.

Europe's history has a strong regional character and many of today's EC member states only acquired their current form during the nineteenth century — Germany and Italy, for example. Defence was often a major issue but the principal characteristic of the current European revolution is that the dissolution of the Soviet Union has also dissolved the major threat to security. Whatever the reason, there is a striking simultaneity about the return of regionalism in the Western part of the Continent.

The politicians and financial market regulators of today may find it surprising that the credit-worthiness of the public sector may be questioned in the future. However, a key element in the credit analysis — the power to print the money which repays public debts — has already been given up, through the Treaty of Maastricht. The other plank of the public sector's credit-worthiness is the power of a large and diversified nation-state to tax its citizens. Europe's history — reflecting geography, culture and language — is based more on smaller regional units than on larger monolithic nation-states.

The examples of Belgium, Italy and Scotland suggest that the vivid examples in the East have rekindled regional sentiment towards self-determination — just at the moment when it is more realistic than at any time for many decades. The EC umbrella will provide some joint security, but a coherent policy is not as imperative as normal because there is an absence of powerful foes, at least for the moment.

With a single money provided by the EC, regional groups will be able to fund worthwhile investment projects easily. Some groups may be tempted to exercise a great degree of self-determination, under the Community umbrella. Inevitably, that freedom will carry the right to pursue unsound financial policies to the point of default. Maintaining the rest of the Community's right to weave its own political tapestry on a canvas of sound money requires careful forethought. However, a broad and strong canvas of Ecu money could support a surprisingly diverse regional tapestry.

## Staying the course

Staying on course for EMU is a key component for a recovery strategy for Europe in the medium term. The potential scale of a single currency serving Europe would make it a rival to the US dollar and be a magnet for savings. The conditions necessary for EMU — price stability and sound public finance — would also encourage savers to take a longer term perspective with their investments. The same conditions should give businessmen the confidence to utilise these savings to make productive investments.

Inevitably, the breakdown of the old system of national currency blocs will not be accomplished without difficulty but there are powerful driving forces — demographics and technology — which would force change even without the push to EMU. The Treaty's rules — combined with the disciplinary effect of the financial markets should prevent public budgets being over-extended even further. The abolition of exchange rate risk within Europe — by locking currencies and eventually moving to a single currency — should enable the private sector to exploit attractive investment opportunities wherever they are located.

---

[1] See *Occupational Pension Schemes in Switzerland — An Emerging New Investment Force,* Salomon Brothers Inc, November 1989.

Chapter Three

# Exploding the Globalisation Myth: Competitive Advantage and Corporate Nationality

## Yao-Su Hu

If, as is being loudly proclaimed, we now live in a "borderless" world dominated by 'global' or 'stateless' corporations, does it make sense to talk of European competitiveness or that of its member states?  In his highly influential *Who is Us?* article, Robert Reich claims that 'us' and American competitiveness should not be defined in terms of American-owned companies but rather in terms of the skills and experience of the American work force.  American companies often produce overseas, while foreign corporations often produce and provide jobs in the US.[1] Using two extreme caricatures, Reich suggests that a foreign company producing in the US may be more 'American' than an American company producing abroad.  Another guru, Kenichi Ohmae, writes:- "It does not matter who builds the factory or who owns the office building or whose money lies behind the shopping mall or whose equity makes the local operation possible.  What matters is that the global corporations ... act as responsible corporate citizens".[2] Not only are firms no longer American, Japanese, Swiss or German, but "if a corporation does not like its government, it can move its headquarters to other, more hospitable places".

In order to combat the intellectual confusion and the sense of helplessness and powerlessness that are engendered by this mode of discourse, this chapter attempts to grapple with three questions:

- Are the 'multinational', 'transnational' or 'global' companies what their names suggest, that is entities that have somehow transcended nations and communities, are indifferent as between them, and have no home nations or bases?  Or are they really national, after all?

• How important are the links between the home base and indigenous corporations for sustaining economic dynamism and international competitiveness?

• To what extent can inward direct foreign investment (DFI) by 'multinationals' based elsewhere be relied upon to solve a nation's competitive problems?

## Corporate nationality versus stateless globalism

In order to answer the first question it is scientifically necessary to adopt a number of objective criteria which could be quantified if the data were available rather than to rely on subjective statements concerning a 'global' mindset, a 'transnational' strategy or a 'polycentric' approach. Here I can only summarise an analytical framework that I have developed elsewhere.[3] There are six elemental criteria (which can be further combined) as follows:

1. *Geographical spread and scope.* For a global company to be indifferent as between nations, a necessary condition is that its operations (as indicated by assets, value-added etc) should be evenly distributed among these nations. Many American multinationals (MNCs) have 60% or more of their operations in the US, while most Japanese MNCs have 80% or more in Japan. The proportion is lower for MNCs from European nations, but even where overseas operations exceed domestic operations, it does not follow that operations in any one foreign nation match those in the home nation. This means that the MNC has more at stake in one country, the home nation, than in any other country or than in all other countries — and that it is therefore in its self-interest, if nothing else, to be most receptive to home-nation interests and pressures. Corporate loyalty is based on self-interest, except perhaps in Anglo-Saxon countries in recent years where the linkage is obscured by arm's length, adversarial relationships between business and the state as well as by the myopic view that the company is a commodity (a bundle of shares to be bought and sold) rather than a community.

2. *Ownership and 3. Control.* With the exception of a handful of binational corporations (such as Shell, Unilever and Asea Brown Boveri) that have two parent companies and hence two home nations, the general pattern with most MNCs is that ownership and control are national (and, by definition, foreign in other countries). They are national at two levels — first with regard to local subsidiaries in foreign countries which are firmly controlled and wholly owned by the parent company, which, second, is itself majority-owned by individual, corporate and institutional

shareholders in the home nation, and inside which ultimate control and decision-making lies in national hands. This pattern has a myriad of profound consequences. It determines who gets the profits from the corporate group as a whole, who has the final say in senior appointments including appointments to local boards and local top management, who awards the 'global mandates' and decides which subsidiary does what, who are the first class citizens in the corporate empire and who are second class, and which currency is the group's home currency (if only because of the currency in which dividends and balance sheets are labelled). It also has many other consequences, some of which are not yet fully understood by the social sciences. Through ownership and control, MNCs are impregnated with the national attributes of the home nation, so that MNCs differ in their goals, strategies and priorities according to whether they are American, Japanese or Swiss. For example, with Anglo-Saxon firms, shareholders come first — with customers and employees a distant second and third. With Japanese companies, employees come first, customers second and shareholders third — and these employees are mainly Japanese employees (if only because they constitute the absolute majority or 80% or more of most Japanese companies' world-wide employment), and the important shareholders are Japanese banks, customers, suppliers, and other companies in a web of cross-shareholdings. These national differences are likely to affect both the way in which international strategy is formulated and the way in which foreign subsidiaries are treated.

*4. People.* A company is not only its capital and operations but also its people. For a global enterprise to have no country to which it owes more loyalty than any other, its management and workforce must be truly 'multinational', evenly distributed between nations and nationalities. What is the reality? The distribution of the workforce as a whole parallels that of the operations of the MNC — which, as we have seen, are centered in the home nation. However, when it comes to top management positions at the corporate headquarters or seats on the parent company's board, the %age of foreigners (non home-nation citizens) is minuscule. General Motors and Ford have no foreigners on their parent boards. Only two non-Americans ever made it to the main board of IBM, and are famous because of that. With Japanese MNCs, there are no foreigners on the main board except at Sony (another renowned exception) and it has been reported that 69% of the senior managers of Japanese subsidiaries in the US are Japanese and that native American managers hit their promotion ceiling soon and are excluded from inner counsels.[4]

*5. Legal nationality.* There is as yet no supranational basis, not even in the European Community, on which a company can come into existence. Companies or corporations are formed under national law and acquire the legal nationality of the country under whose law they are incorporated. Within an MNC, the parent company has the legal nationality of the home nation, the foreign subsidiaries of the respective host nations. The parent and subsidiaries are subject to the jurisdiction of national law, and it is a travesty to portray them as having transcended nation-states. Legal nationality also raises a number of interesting legal issues, such as the conflict of laws, the extra-territorial application of national laws, and whether a company is entitled to diplomatic protection (which requires, under well-established rules of international law, the existence of a real and effective link between the corporation and the nation, evidence of which could be ownership or control, in addition to legal nationality which is simply a matter of place of incorporation). Should Japanese automobile transplants in the US enjoy full American diplomatic protection in the event of a conflict with the EC?

*6. Tax domicile.* The local subsidiary of a foreign corporation is taxed by the host government on its local earnings; manipulation of transfer pricing between the local subsidiary and its sister and parent companies can reduce locally attributable earnings. The home government of an MNC does not have this problem because it can, if it so chooses, tax the worldwide earnings of the group as a whole by virtue of the fact that the subsidiaries' earnings belong to the parent and because it has access to the consolidated accounts of the parent and of the group. With home-based MNCs, not only is the tax base higher but the scope for tax avoidance or evasion is smaller.

**Applying the criteria: the nature of the beast?**

Applying the six criteria together, we find that, apart from the few binational corporations, there is no such thing as a true 'multinational', 'transnational', 'global' or 'stateless' firm in the sense which the terms intend to convey, of an entity that has transcended nation-states. There are only national firms with foreign, international operations.

Corporate nationality (or national character) goes beyond any single dimension such as ownership (the bogey of Reich and Ohmae) or legal nationality. It results from a combination of the criteria and their inter-relationships as applied to the parent and subsidiary companies.

In addition to the fact that the binationals are based in Europe, MNCs based in European nations tend to be more internationalised than their American and Japanese counterparts. The share of assets and operations located in the home nation tends to be lower, though the share located in Western Europe is comparable to US and Japanese groups. European MNCs also tend to be more internationalised in their senior posts. German companies, with their dual board structure, often have one Swiss and one Dutch national as members of their supervisory boards. Nestlé has an all-Swiss board but a number of non-Swiss senior managers (Germans can be accepted as honorary Swiss citizens). The greater internationalisation of MNCs based in Europe results from geographical factors — the relatively small size of the home nation compared to the US or Japan, geographical proximity between neighbouring European nations — and cultural and linguistic factors, as well as the process of European integration which increasingly means that the home market, though not (yet?) the home nation, is the EC itself.

### Applying the criteria: who is us?

When everyone is equal, some are more equal than others. Within a multinational group there is a home government and hence there is a home nation, a home government and a home tax authority. Usually the bulk of assets and operations is located in the home nation, and the majority of the owners, managers, workers and senior decision-makers are citizens of the home nation. It stands to reason that the major share of the profits, tax revenues and best jobs accrue to the home nation or its citizens at home or abroad. A national firm with international operations is 'one of us'.

Investment abroad is healthy if it goes hand-in-hand with upgrading and progress at home, so that it is the less productive, lower value-added jobs and activities that are moved abroad. Furthermore, it is often not possible to penetrate foreign markets without at least some investment in selling and servicing: the much-publicised amount of intra-firm trade between nations could be due as much to DFI in sales and services as to DFI in assembly and manufacturing. On the other hand, investment abroad that transfers the more productive jobs and activities to other nations indicates that there is something wrong with the company or the home nation — or both.

### Applying the criteria: moving the company?

It is wrong to think that companies can move easily from one country to another. It is one thing to shift the legal address of the group's holding company (which must be authorised by the two governments concerned on pain of severe tax penalties). It is another thing, difficult but not impossible, to locate abroad the home base for a particular segment, business or product line, especially when it results from new investments or the acquisition of a foreign company. But if a company has 60% or more of its assets, operations and people in one country, it is hard to see how it could transfer the 60% wholesale to another home base. Stepping up capital expenditures in foreign subsidiaries and acquiring foreign companies help to decrease the proportion of the home base in the worldwide total, but this takes time. It may take a decade to change a few percentage points. And the process may also divert attention from upgrading competitive advantage at home.

## Implications for dynamism and competitiveness

I now turn to the second question posed at the start of this chapter. What are the fundamental sources of competitive advantage for nations and their firms? With post-World War II decolonisation, reductions in transportation costs, the increasing use of synthetic substitutes and the decreasing ratio of raw material costs to the value of final outputs, access or unequal access to raw materials has almost disappeared as a source of competitive advantage. With post-war liberalisation in many fields, unequal access to markets and to DFI opportunities (emphasised by Lenin in his time) has been greatly reduced in importance for advanced nations and their firms — with the admittedly great exception of access to the Japanese market for non-Japanese firms. Low labour costs are a transient advantage — there is always somewhere cheaper — and must be combined with organisation and technology to translate into an actual advantage.

Today, the sources of advantage are much more subtle and intangible. Writing more than 25 years ago in *Le Défi Américain*, Servan-Schreiber drew attention to the immaterial nature of sources of wealth — ability, organisation, aptitude, talent, spirit, intelligence, will and, last but not least, autonomy or the power to make final, integrated decisions at the strategic level, without which there is no real risk-taking and hence no high rewards. The over-arching message of Michael Porter's *The Competitive Advantage of Nations* (1990) is that competitive advantage grows out of continuous, relentless improvement, upgrading and innovation. Other schools of thought, from Friedrich List to the present day, emphasize the importance of human capital, which we must understand to be not only individual capital but also collective capital embodied in groups, institutions, communities and nations.

For healthy companies (including big 'multinationals' but by no means confined to them) and healthy nations, the home nation (or even the localities within the home nation) is the primary source of the firm's international competitive advantage. There are at least two basic reasons for this. The first lies in the relativity of advantage. By establishing a local presence in Germany, for example, an American corporation may be able to tap into German advantages or sources of advantages. But it is unlikely to be able to tap them better than German firms and players. Secondly, there may be attitudinal barriers to transferring skills and ideas from the German operation of the US company back to its home base and headquarters. Tapping into another nation's sources of advantages, unless the home base were to be really moved, can help to reduce disadvantages or supplement home-based advantages. By itself it cannot, by definition, provide an edge relative to native players based in more dynamic nations. Competition may be global, but this does not mean that the sources of competitive advantage have become global.

One key indicator of this home nation effect is the geographical locus of R&D activities. R&D is only part of the much wider process of innovation but it is relatively easy to identify (or would be were more data to become readily available). Where R&D is carried out is where innovation takes place, since the former is an indispensable component of the latter. For most multinationals, R&D is even more disproportionately concentrated in the home base than the firm's assets, operations or total employees. A sample of German MNCs in 1983 had 65% of total employment located at home, but 83% of their R&D personnel.[5] In 1991 the German giant, Siemens, had 60% of its total employees in Germany, but 75% of its R&D personnel. Even in more globally oriented Britain, Glaxo, a leading pharmaceutical firm, had in 1992 only one third of its total workforce in the UK but 58% of R&D manpower. Or take one of the most extreme cases of internationalisation, Philips Electronics, which has only 15% of its assets in the Netherlands but some 40% of its R&D. Research at SPRU, based on the patenting data of the world's largest 600 plus firms, shows that Japanese firms carry out 99% of their technological activities at home, American firms 92%, French, German and Italian firms 85 to 88%, UK and Swiss firms around 55%, with the lowest proportions for Dutch and Belgian firms (around 40%).[6]

The nation where a company's main R&D effort takes place indicates where the heart of its innovation drive lies. Real innovation is centered in the home nation because this is where all the elements required for strategic, integrated and final decision-making, both within the company and in terms of its external relations with the most important customers, suppliers, bankers, financiers, research or university centres, as well as with the home government, are present. In innovative activities, the home nation is the locomotive, assuming a role out of proportion to its weight in total operations.

This home nation effect means that higher-order activities (such as R&D, design, engineering, product planning, advanced production and central decision-making) are located in the home nation and usually as close as possible to the firm's headquarters and main facilities. These are the activities that require the greatest skill-intensity, create the greatest value-added, pay the highest compensation, carry the most prestige, power and responsibility, and (as contrasted with branch plant operations) are the least prone to sudden cutbacks or to being moved offshore. "They are therefore the most beneficial to local employees and to surrounding society, in terms of everything from retail spending power to the stimulation of higher education through the demand for graduate employees and research."[7]

With healthy companies based in healthy home nations, the home nation effect also means that exports of relatively more advanced products, parts and components will take place from the home nation, both to third-party buyers and to wholly or majority-owned subsidiaries abroad. Manufacturing subsidiaries abroad will also purchase technology, machinery and processes from the parent company or suppliers in the home nation. A recent study has found that foreign-owned subsidiaries in Japan and the US import more from parents than they buy locally: trade is tightly linked to investment, and corporate nationality matters.[8] Foreign companies may, under special circumstances, make a host nation their home base for a particular business segment or product line, but their home nations remain their home bases for the corporate group as a whole.

**The role of inward direct foreign investment**

Assessing the effects of inward DFI is an extremely complicated affair which seldom leads to any clear-cut conclusions because it depends on the different questions being asked, on what is assumed would have happened or will happen in the absence of the DFI (which itself depends on government policies and the dynamism of indigenous enterprises), and on the level or unit of analysis — in other words, DFI by a single firm or in aggregate, and the effects on the respective locality, nation or region.

Consider the case of IBM, a leading multinational in a most strategic industry. It has been renowned, justly so, for its good corporate citizenship in Europe and for undertaking R&D in European host nations. Yet it has been estimated that IBM's R&D intensity (R&D personnel as a percentage of total employees) was half in Europe to that in the USA. As I have argued above, the MNC contributes more to its home nation than to any other nation, and relying solely on a foreign MNC cannot be expected to bring the host economy to the level and pace of the nation in which the MNC is based. However, IBM probably did contribute significantly to upgrading and improvement in Europe's computer industries both directly, through its operations, which must be reckoned to be part of the European industry at least in a geographical sense, and indirectly, by educating end-users and by stimulating indigenous rivals and suppliers.

The American challenge has now been replaced by the Japanese challenge. Let us again consider the two most high profile industries, electronics and automobiles. For Hitachi, the Japanese electronics giant, it has been reported that research abroad is still insignificant compared to the scale of its efforts at home: the UK laboratory in Cambridge employed five researchers, the Irish centre in Dublin 12, and the US facility in San Francisco 10, compared to around 4000 scientists in its nine Japanese laboratories.[9] In the automotive industry, Toyota, Nissan and Honda have each established one or two development centres in Belgium, Germany and the UK. However, these are very small operations (reportedly employing less than 80 engineers each) and, moreover, Japanese engineers accounted for three quarters of the total at each.[10]

Most other Japanese industries do practically no R&D in European host economies. Most Japanese subsidiaries in Europe can be viewed as sales, distribution and servicing operations which have recently begun to undertake production activities to ward off protectionist measures. More often than not, however, the latter are assembly operations, which means firstly that they import key components (for example, engines and gearboxes for cars) from the home nation, secondly that local value-added or local content is low, and, thirdly, that employment consists mainly of low-skilled, direct labour.[11] More precise figures are available from the US. Japanese subsidiaries in the USA import nearly three times the components that European affiliates do as a proportion of final sales value, according to a 1990 Commerce Department survey.[12] This is inevitable as long as the strategic core of the innovative effort of Japanese firms lies in Japan. As volume cars are being transplanted to the US and Europe, the Japanese labour force graduates to higher value-added and higher technology models such as the Infiniti and the Lexus.

Let us now turn to the experience of host economies. Within the EC, the Republic of Ireland has led the way in basing its strategy for economic development on attracting inward DFI through very generous tax exemptions and various grants and incentives. However, according to the OECD (1985) this has led to the emergence of a dual economy. Foreign subsidiaries have developed few linkages with the indigenous economy, have contributed little in the way of local research or technology, and depend heavily on imported raw materials and components. Furthermore the financial costs of the incentives were considerable. Despite the employment created by the foreign subsidiaries, the unemployment rate in Ireland remains one of the highest in the EC.

According to Porter, widespread inward DFI in the UK carries the message that the process of competitive upgrading is not entirely healthy; indigenous firms lack the capabilities to defend their market positions against foreign firms. These investments have been driven mainly by low wages, take the form of assembly activities and have limited potential for upgrading the economy. In the past the UK has attracted a disproportionate share of US and Japanese DFI into the EC; in the last year it has encouraged MNCs such as Hoover and Johnson to relocate production activities from France to the UK. This focus on cheap labour is just the opposite of the kind of thinking that is required to build up long-term dynamism and competitive advantage.

Scotland's 'Silicon Glen', based mainly on the local activities of American MNCs, has failed to spawn a vibrant electronics industry capable of autonomous, self-sustaining growth, and these branch plants tend to be the first to go when the parent runs into problems. Spinoffs and startups have not happened on a significant scale. One reason is the nature of the jobs being created by the MNCs. Almost all the jobs are blue-collar. Young, low-paid workers simply screw together components imported from the US or the Far East. Key activities such as research, engineering and upper-level management remain at corporate headquarters. Scottish employees do not gain the ability to strike out on their own.[13] Another reason is that entrepreneurship, whether of the high-tech, low-tech or no-tech variety, is a social and cultural phenomenon, and qualified people in Scotland and elsewhere in the EC may prefer working for big companies rather than for themselves or for startups.

**Multinational future**

What can we conclude? Inward DFI may indeed provide economic benefits. However, it is unrealistic to rely on it as the sole engine of upgrading and growth. In a dynamic economy, a vibrant indigenous sector is what attracts foreign MNCs in the first place; it is also what maximises the benefits from inward DFI. Local dynamism attracts higher value-added activities, maximises linkages and spill-over effects, and challenges effectively what might otherwise have been monopoly rents for the MNCs. If the conditions for economic dynamism are unfavourable, it is not the task of foreigners to put them right.

Meanwhile, competitive bidding between nations and their localities for inward DFI is very costly and self-defeating. Within the EC, the bidders reason that if they lose, they not only lose the jobs but will see hoped-for exports turn into imports. At the overall level of the EC, however, everybody loses. Costly incentives use up scarce taxpayer's money which could have been used to alleviate tax burdens on indigenous firms, to promote small and medium enterprises and entrepreneurship, to build advanced infrastructure and factors of production, or otherwise to enhance competitive advantage and dynamism.

Global, stateless, multinational companies are not what their names suggest. They are national (or binational) firms with international operations. They bring disproportionate benefits to their home countries, but they need a healthy home environment in order to continuously upgrade and improve. Countries needs home-based firms just as the firm needs its home base. If the economy is healthy, inward DFI can add to dynamism, but they can seldom, if ever, substitute completely for home-based enterprises or act as the sole engine of growth. Dynamism and competitive advantage require continuous improvement, upgrading and innovation, a long-term process that depends on what Porter calls the 'diamond' — that is, long-term supply and demand conditions, the creation of advanced, higher-order factors of production including human capital and the research base, stimulus from the demand side especially from advanced users, stimulus from related and supplying industries, and the commitment and drive of firms which require healthy rivalry and competition. Apart from being open to new ideas and technology from anywhere in the world, Europe also needs to have a higher share of its trade — both exports and imports — with the most dynamic region in the world, which is Pacific Asia, and to invest more there, so that more of that Asian dynamism can be transmitted to Europe.

[1] *Harvard Business Review* January/February 1990.
[2] *The Borderless World* London: Collins 1990.
[3] 'Global or stateless corporations are national firms with international operations' in *California Management Review*, Winter 1992.
[4] L. Thurow *Head to Head* New York: William Morrow 1992, pp 121-122.
[5] M. Wortmann 'Multinationals and the internationalization of R&D' in *Research Policy*, April 1990.
[6] Pari Patel *Localized production of technology for the global market* University of Sussex: SPRU, February 1993.
[7] C. Lorenz 'Why nationality can matter' in *Financial Times*, 20 June 1988.
[8] D. Encarnation *Rivals Beyond Trade* Cornell University Press, 1992.
[9] *Financial Times*, 3 December 1990.
[10] A. Graves 'Globalization of the automobile industry' in C. Freeman et al *Technology and the Future of Europe*, London: Pinter, 1991.
[11] B.G. James *Trojan Horse* London: Mercury, 1989.
[12] 'Why corporate nationality matters' in *Business Week*, 12 July 1993.
[13] 'Silicon Glen saga' in *Business Week*, 9 October 1989.

Chapter Four

# The New Industrial Dimension

## Christopher Wilkinson [1]

Industrial policies in the European Community during the coming decade face a dilemma between the long term objective of building on the achievements of the Community and the short term constraints arising from the recession and the still unresolved divergence between the policies and economies of member states. The last twenty years' development of European industrial policy should now be coming to fruition but, at the same time, major obstacles stand in the way of taking full advantage of that success. At the best of times, European policies take years to develop and implement because they have to take account of the need for transition between different starting points in the individual member states. This aspect has to be re-emphasised today because of the plans for further enlargement and the intention to cooperate with Central and Eastern Europe.

In theory the Community should be on the threshold of an unprecedented economic base to develop its industrial objectives in terms of open domestic and international markets giving Europe the opportunity to concentrate on the areas where it can be most successful. In practice, however, these potential advantages are prejudiced by the continuing recession, the threat of further monetary instability, the delay in finalising the Uruguay Round (and the concomitant reluctance to address problems of EC commercial policy).

As a result, Community industrial policy suffers. That which ought to be a stable and long term vision of Europe making the best of its attributes tends to be blurred by a short term, defensive approach where the main question is how to respond to more successful competitors abroad. While not denying the weight and urgency of some of these short-term constraints, this chapter attempts to address the longer term objectives of European industrial policy in terms of a few basic ideas. These include:

- building on the internal market;

- a dynamic and innovative industrial structure;

- meeting social and environmental needs;

- education and training for industrial development;

- trade policy after the Uruguay Round.

The arguments that follow have to be read from that perspective in order to grasp the need for a quiet radical transition during the coming years. This is particularly the case given that the uncertainties referred to above will require a flexible and robust industrial strategy able to accommodate significant changes in the future structure of the labour force, the conditions of international competition and the price and availability of energy and other resources.

## Building on the Single Market

The internal market programme initiated under the auspices of Lord Cockfield has now been largely put in place. It was, however, always clear that the direct harmonisation of a wide range of technical regulations, standards and regulatory conditions would not be enough to ensure that European industry was able to take full advantage of the potential scale and prosperity of the European and international markets. There is still a long way to go in achieving a fully integrated EC economy. There are still many problems and delays in actually putting into effect EC directives in all member states, and the Commission will have to act on this aspect, if necessary, through legal and political pressure. The communications infrastructures also need substantial investment if they are to support a Europe-wide economy. As a result, many companies, particularly the smaller ones, cannot yet take full advantage of the theoretical results of the internal market programme.

Meanwhile, however, the European economy is becoming an extremely favourable area of operations for those large companies which have the managerial, technological and financial resources to operate at a continental and even global scale. A large proportion of such firms are of US or Japanese origin. Those companies of European origin which are able to operate at the European level retain nonetheless strong national characteristics and tend to establish their European scope through acquisition and merger rather than expansion into new markets.

The 'big is beautiful' approach carries its own risks: in some sectors they are grave. Take, for example, the high technology industries, where there is — for a variety of reasons — a dearth of new entrants. The computing industry is perhaps the best example. Given that the larger and longer established companies will ultimately decline through rationalisation, restructuring and occasional major errors, the result is a weak industrial structure. A primary objective, therefore, would be to encourage directly the creation and expansion of smaller and newer companies to become economically viable as quickly as possible, and then to encourage their expansion into cross-border European operations. Depending on the situation in specific sectors it would also be desirable to encourage new entrants and particularly to lower the barriers to entry across national borders.

The main lines of an effective industrial policy for smaller companies have been identified and are widely known. They include factors such as financing, training, access to technology and the necessary communications networks and services.

Against this objective there is the growing concern that given the size and resources of a number of American and Japanese corporations, the Community's industrial policy should be to encourage the creation of comparably competitive organisations essentially by relaxing competition policy. The approach to growth through mergers, however, is inherently risky and should be pursued with great caution. In the first place there are already quite a few very large companies in Europe — although they never seem to be big enough. Secondly, such mergers may give rise to unforeseen management difficulties which prejudice the anticipated results. Thirdly, the resulting organisations may still not be able to compete internationally under prevailing conditions. And, fourthly, this approach, which may yet be a last resort in certain cases, still does nothing to encourage the development of new entrants into these industries.

In practice some of the most 'strategic' mergers which can be envisaged involve vertical integration within a given sector of activity, of which the most topical examples are in communications: equipment, network operation, provision of services, media and date bases. For reasons of policy — competition and information policy notably — the desirability of such mergers is debatable. It would be unfortunate if, in order to counteract growing concentration among American and Japanese companies in these fields, the Community decided to permit mergers and acquisitions which were opposed to its basic interests.

In such a case there is a prospect of the internal market not only benefiting disproportionately non-European companies, but also leading to a highly concentrated structure in European industry as the larger companies respond to the opportunities of the Common Market and to foreign competition by merging and rationalising their existing activities.

As a general proposition, the Community should — other things being equal — continue to pursue an essentially open and non-protectionist trade policy. It will be increasingly important to ensure across a wide range of policies that no unnecessary barriers are created to the entry of new European companies into markets which in the normal course of events may become increasingly concentrated, sometimes mainly to the benefit of non-European companies. As will be seen below, in addition to trade policy considerations this approach has implications for standardisation policy, protection of intellectual property rights and the right of establishment.

The completion of the internal market for services is another critical area of concern. Broadly speaking, companies which offer services in one member state have the right to offer the same services in another, subject to a limited number of restrictions which can be invoked in the public interest. In practice, however, it is precisely these service sectors which have been most heavily regulated by national government. Although these sectors are generally in the process of deregulation and privatisation, it is still moot whether the process will really give European companies effective new opportunities in each other's traditional markets — particularly as their international competitors are also well placed by virtue of the same internal market rules to offer services across EC borders.

The Treaty provides for a very open European market conferring virtually automatic most-favoured-nation treatment on any foreign company which has an operation registered in any one of the member states. This, together with a *prima facie* right to offer services throughout the EC based on services provided in any member state may lead to a very rapid opening of the previously regulated services markets to international competition — and possibly before the European service providers are able to move to take advantage of the new situation themselves. This also raises the question of whether the Community's international partners afford anything like the same degree of market access to European companies, a question to which most observers would respond negatively.

A second area of concern is the weakness and limitations of Community infrastructure. Air space is highly congested but regional air services are poor and expensive; the high-speed railway network has made little progress outside France; there are serious deficiencies in the advanced telecommunications networks of all kinds and lacunae in the energy supply networks which contribute to high costs and inefficiencies. Even the now relatively well-developed motorway network is operating under considerable stress in several parts of the EC, partly as a direct result of the inadequacies of other components of Europe's communications infrastructure.

In this context, it must be recognised that in the contemporary economy, physical transport is only part of the industrial system, and that high quality communication of information, images and other data is equally if not more important. This is particularly so because communications technology now permits a much more sophisticated use of the media for forms of entertainment and education than has previously been considered possible. These advantages can be extended to many traditional sectors of activity such as publishing, transport and health care, among others. The basic requirements of this new interactive 'multi-media' industry will be high capacity communications networks (based usually on optical fibre), significant computing power in the domestic terminals (including future generations of television sets) and access to a wide range of information in the form of data bases and digitalised audio-visual material.

The technology of this new industry will be global, and will be applied in the United States in the near future by companies some of which already have interests in the Community. The preconditions for successful European participation in the industry will be the availability of the high capacity infrastructure and a profitable market. To ensure that the potential benefits are quickly and widely available, one should also consider instigating the equivalent of universal services to home and businesses based on open standards available to all potential entrants to these markets, and easy and affordable use of information. The latter point is important because multi-media in Europe will be able to draw on a vast cultural heritage which can be transferred to digital electronic data bases for widespread use in education, entertainment and other activities. If these unique sources of information were to become monopolised by the service providers which first enter these markets, the opportunities afforded by the Single Market to homes and business could be put at risk. Rather, such services should be treated as a common asset to industry as a whole. Conditions of use of such information, including remuneration for it, should be such as to make it available in electronic media but not to restrict access to specific service providers or users.

**Research and technology**

The objectives of Community policies for research and development are not exclusively concerned with industrial policy. Support for fundamental and basic research is oriented more towards ensuring a continuing resource of scientific excellence in Europe, given the massive and often unpredictable contribution of science to European society during the past 250 years. The EC's interest in nuclear fusion is a very large speculative investment into a possible solution to the double prejudice of contemporary energy —

global warming through carbon dioxide emissions and the waste problem arising from nuclear fission.

With regard to the industrial dimension of EC R&D policy, the EC Framework Programmes are devoted to cooperative, precompetitive industrial research in a number of identified fields. The Community finances the costs of cross-border cooperation between companies and universities.

This concept was first developed in the ESPRIT information technology programme, and has since been applied to communications and manufacturing technologies. To date, the results of these efforts have been mixed. Broadly speaking, the desired level of European cooperation has been achieved, and has become a model for other forms of cooperation, including the intergovernmental Eureka programme. But the industrial results have left a lot to be desired. There would appear to be two basic reasons for this. First, the ostensibly 'pre-competitive' nature of the research has discouraged activity directed to ensuring that research results would be applied (except in certain standardisation work). Second, notwithstanding the declared strategic character of the research, some of the larger companies seem to have retained their critical research priorities for their own in-house projects. It is proving to be very difficult to avoid falling between these two stools.

It is consistent with this trend, if discouragingly so, that EC activities concerned with the diffusion and utilisation of research results comprise only a modest and somewhat detached part of the Framework Programme. It is now desirable to demystify the concept of pre-competitive research — and to concentrate at EC level on ensuring that R&D results are exploited in the market place and made quickly available to other companies. Unless this happens, much of the human and financial effort put into European R&D will be wasted. A growing number of US and Japanese firms have access to all their parent companies' technological resources for their operations in Europe.

**Human resources for competitiveness and employment**

In a modern economy human resources are more important in the long term than capital and material resources. The ability to use information productively is becoming the most important human resource of all. The EC economy is organised on the basis of freedom of movement and liberal enterprise, but its principle benefits will not be realised unless there are motivated and qualified people, especially in the younger generations, who are able to enter the market with new products and services based on new ideas. This is particularly so in the newer high technology branches of the economy such as information, electronics, biochemistry and materials, among others.

Consequently, improving education and training in the population at large, and among the young and the unemployed in particular, is a major objective of industrial policy — quite apart from its social and individual benefits. The persistence of this objective is reinforced by the realisation that European demography is with a few exceptions going through a period of stability, if not decline. It will be all the more vital to ensure that the education of the younger and smaller cohorts of the population is optimised. If society as a whole is to sustain a high living standard and the social protection to which current generations have become accustomed, it will become essential that those in full time activity will be able to produce much higher value-added individually and collectively than in the past.

These objectives need to be tackled on a broad front. Although the implementation of education and training policies is going to take place through national and regional organisations, the priority and content of the policy has to be agreed and, if necessary, supported financially, by the EC. Failure in this area would be too dangerous for all the other objectives of Community policy which are based on a prosperous and internationally competitive economy.

Although the main lines of consistent policy in this regard have been described many times before, the current disinterest in technology-related skills (at least in certain member states), the number of long-term unemployed and the limited employment opportunities for recent graduates all testify to the fact that this problem is far from being solved.

Effective steps must be taken to ensure longer full time education and training, and to offer a more diverse range of educational opportunities prior to entering the labour force. It will be necessary furthermore to target the groups most likely to drop out of the educational and training system including the unemployed, the illiterate and those who have not acquired a basic education at school. Finally, continuing training opportunities should be created for older people, since given demographic trends, they may well wish to remain active later in life. The effective participation of industry is also a priority, but until the end of the current recession it is a bit much to expect industry to solve an issue of public policy for which governments have yet to find a solution themselves.

## Innovation and competitiveness

If the Community's current R&D policy is to succeed, it will have to be bolstered by an innovation policy that addresses the question of access to and use of the results of the EC research programmes. There have been several attempts during the past decade or more to develop an industrial innovation policy for the EC, often linked to the promotion of smaller enterprises. There are two fundamental strands to innovation policy. First, the policy has to be polyvalent, drawing on the impact of several discrete policy areas and budgets, including regional policy, competition policy and standardisation, as well as R&D. Second, the policy has to be highly decentralised in order to reach the whole range of European companies. There has to be, therefore, a high level of coordination between the Commission and other institutions, including the EIB, and a high degree of consensus among member governments as to the objectives and methods of the innovation policy. At the very least, it would require all member states to create and maintain an organisational support structure for small and medium-sized enterprises.

## Social and environmental needs

Industrial policy is directed to ensuring that the needs of the people are met today and in the long term. That means that the economic system not only has to offer jobs to those who want to work, but also has to be geared to fulfilling people's expectations of European civilisation — which usually means a sustainable life-style. This problem is now acute for two reasons. First, the recession has exposed areas of basic need, particularly among the poor and unemployed, which ought to have been tackled some time ago. Thus, basic housing and minimal amenities are lacking for a significant and perhaps growing portion of the European population. Second, many improvements are now necessary to increase the energy efficiency of the household and to reduce pollution and waste in industry. The energy economy is especially vulnerable to the end of the recession because demand for petroleum products will escalate once again with unpredictable consequences for price and supply.

The following elements emerge from an industrial point of view in the fields of housing, recycling and conservation:

> • Member governments should each undertake to ensure that everyone has a warm, dry home with access to adequate public transport. The EC's cohesion and regional funds could be used to finance this. The effect on the building industry and its suppliers would be dramatic in terms of new house building, repair and

renovation. Although few building jobs are unskilled, most of the necessary skills either exist in the labour market today or can be acquired relatively easily and quickly. In Northern Europe, this policy could be associated with a special emphasis on home insulation and fuel efficiency.

• It will also be necessary to pay increasing attention to the recovery and reuse of resources. Whereas recycling of glass and paper is already widespread and could be made universal without great difficulties, the separation, recovery and recycling of much waste plastic is also technically possible — and should be promoted strongly. However, there are other problems whose solution will be much more difficult. Wrecked and unserviceable motor cars, broken-down domestic appliances, obsolete consumer electronic products and computing equipment are all being discarded, dumped and not recycled. It is not only a question of the significant volume of carbon tetrafluoride in the cooling systems of refrigerators and the plastic casings of most appliances. The electronics involved include some valuable products and a few dangerous ones. Such dumped waste is virtually undegradeable. A washing machine will rust away; a television or a computer will not.

It is clear that the practice of planned obsolescence and a certain reluctance in some sectors to introduce contemporary technology into products is prejudicial to the rational use of resources. On the contrary, starting with those sectors where technology is stabilising, such as domestic appliances and motor cars, it is essential that the products on the market are as durable and efficient as the available technology permits — and at an affordable price. This is all the more pertinent because industrial automation is progressively eliminating employment in the manufacture of mass consumer products. It would be more desirable for jobs to be created in maintenance and recycling than in artificially labour-intensive manufacturing. It cannot, after all, be denied that a large proportion of these products, including cars, consumer electronics and computers, are going to be imported in any case or assembled in Europe in robotised factories owned by US and Japanese companies.

These issues can only be resolved by a combination of market pricing, regulation and public opinion. Civic education about an energy efficient economy is needed. Simply legislating more EC directives would certainly fail to be effective, quite apart from the current unpopularity of such an approach. And short sighted market considerations will not give the right signals to the public either, particularly during the recession. The social and environmental priorities for future industrial policy will without doubt generate employment at levels of skill that are readily available. This strategy will also benefit from an element of natural protection, although there will be some international trade in waste reprocessing. On the other hand, international trade rules must quickly recognise that the costs of recycling products in the computing and consumer electronics fields are a legitimate charge on manufacturers and importers.

## Trade policy

Discussion of international trade policy has focussed inevitably but disproportionately on whether the GATT Uruguay Round would be finally adopted on the basis of the Draft Final Agreement proposed nearly three years ago. The exorbitant delay in reaching any decision has had two major drawbacks. First, the concentration on the negotiations about agriculture has diverted attention from a fundamental problem concerning American trade policy. This lies in several provisions of US law which authorise, and in some instances oblige the Administration to discriminate among and even retaliate against US trade partners on a bilateral basis. These provisions fly in the face of the general GATT principle of most-favoured-nation treatment, and are a reserve power of negotiation on the Uruguay Round that no other trading power claims. Unsurprisingly, US negotiators continue to seek exceptions from the MFN principle, particularly for trade in services. There is every indication that neither the US Congress nor the Clinton Administration will be prepared to waive these powers even under a multilateral agreement that met US desiderata in all other respects. The Americans deem these powers to be essential to lever trade concessions from Japan, but they have not forborne to use or threaten to use these retaliatory powers against the EC.

This leaves the Community in an invidious position. If it seeks to make an issue out of the Americans' non-GATT trade powers, it risks creating, in addition to agriculture, another problematical dossier. That may well provoke Congress into rejecting any agreement. On the other hand, the EC's own trade policy instruments are comparatively weak, and the procedures to make them apply are such that the Community has rarely, if ever agreed to act decisively on a unilateral basis, and has continued to prefer the multilateral disciplines of GATT. This is likely to continue to be the case after the Uruguay Round.

The second problem is that the agenda of the Uruguay Round is now thoroughly out of date. For some time trade problems have occurred in areas not addressed by GATT. The key problem areas are technology, environment, competition and social policies. These can be summarised as follows:

- **Technology**. Governmental or corporate strategies to target the development of certain technologies can distort the conditions of international trade. Other countries are now seeking to compensate against unfair advantage by adopting similar strategies themselves or by trade protection. Would it not be more desirable to establish a base line of high technology transfer between otherwise free-trading partners? For example, should the technology included in international standards be available as of right to all competitors worldwide?

- **Targetting**. Technological targeting by Japan (MITI), the United States (DOD, DARPA) and the European Community (Ariane, Airbus) are a fact of life. But there is no consensus about how they should be dealt with when they give rise to trade friction.

- **Environment**. The more robust environment policies of the future will clearly have important trade implications internationally. Environment is already an issue within the EC and NAFTA.

- **Competition**. In the field of competition policy, the conflict is mainly between Japan and the rest of the world. The Japanese government continues to promote extensive cooperation between major corporations as well as the integration of a wide range of related activities in single companies. The anti-competitive effects clearly spill over into third markets. It is urgent to contain the international consequences of industrial concentration in Japan if Europe is to avoid an unnecessary and undesirable degree of concentration motivated solely on the need to try to compete with Japanese conglomerates.

- **Working conditions**. In the interests of EC employment objectives and, ultimately in respect of human rights, it is necessary to establish a link between the objectives of free trade and the basic working conditions prevailing in developing and newly industrialising countries now entering world markets for manufactured products. Europeans know only too well the depths to which health and safety conditions can sink at the work place. We should not be complicit in replicating the working conditions of Europe's 19th century industrial revolution in Asia, Africa and Latin America in the 21st.

All these problems are upon us now.

---

[1] This chapter reflects the personal views of the author and does not necessarily reflect the policies of the EC Commission.

# Chapter Five

# Information Networking for the New Economy

## Ian Mackintosh

The next stages of European integration, if they happen at all, will require for their implementation vastly better pan-European communications than exist at present. This is not simply a matter of ensuring the (reasonably) free movement of goods by the provision of improved physical links such as road and rail, equivalent to the region's arteries and veins. It is clear that standardised procedures, documentation and data will also be essential to the integration process. Only by creating pervasive and cheap communication systems for the free movement of information will it be possible to put into effect harmonised Community policies in areas such as trade, law enforcement, medical services, social and employment provisions and much else besides.

In this prospective New Europe, then, eventual success will depend on the development of a European "neural network" to carry the vast quantities of data and voice traffic which will flow between the dispersed and diverse member states. To meet this need, Europe will have to create a pervasive new electronic communications network, originally dubbed 'Eurogrid', sometimes referred to as the 'European Nervous System' and which President Delors recently christened 'the information infrastructure'.[1]

## Building the Eurogrid

The use of fibre-optic technology for inter-city and international telecommunications is already *de rigueur*, of course, and has come about because of the early recognition by the Public Telecommunications Operators (PTOs) that this is a powerful tool for reducing the costs of long-distance telecommunication links. But that is not enough to meet the needs of the New Europe. What is required is the provision of such broadband connections — that is, capable of carrying massive amounts of voice and data traffic, very cheaply — to every home, office, school and hospital in the Community, all linked by means of standard communication protocols and terminating on compatible 'black boxes', or terminals. By this means, with totally transparent frontiers and at minimal cost, company will do business with company using multi-media techniques of communication such as electronic mail, Electronic Data Interchange (EDI), Office Document Architecture (ODA), Electronic Funds Transfer (EFT) and many others. In the same way, government office will talk unto government office, medical centre will consult with specialist practitioner and university researcher will compare notes with his or her counterparts elsewhere. This new order will also affect the home front, where far-flung relatives will stay in touch through the medium of affordable, high-quality video telephones and extensive interactive entertainment services will be on tap.

All of this is already technically feasible, of course, but the costs of installing broadband connections to each home and office — the so-called 'local loop' — are perceived to be very high. This accounts for the fact that none of the European PTOs has so far shown much enthusiasm for making local-loop investments other than for business customers clustered efficiently in city centres. On the other hand, it needs to be said, cable TV companies seem undaunted by the financial risk of digging up urban streets in order to lay broadband cables at our curbside, and both the United States and Japanese governments are now actively encouraging investments in what Vice-President Gore has called "information highways". In short, Europe is once again falling behind the rest of the industrialised world in reaping the fruits of the electronics revolution and, once again, all for the sake of the right combination of vision and money — in the right hands.

However, it is not just the availability of pervasive communication networks on which the future prosperity of Europe depends: it is also the power of electronics technology — which underwrites the entire information technology (IT) revolution — to create jobs in IT and to provide operating efficiencies which are essential to establishing global competitiveness in a host of IT-dependent industrial and commercial activities.

For example, in coming into existence, Eurogrid will itself represent a huge and enduring market for IT products and services. There will be not only the requirements of the network itself but also the massive demand for the hardware and software used in the wide variety of IT terminals which will be required at user sites to access and use the network. The value of the services which the grid will carry, and the revenues which will accrue to the network providers, will be similarly enormous.

To put some flesh on these bones, in round figures we are talking about an 'enabling' network investment by the European PTOs of around $400 billion spread over 20 years or so, on which they will eventually enjoy annual revenues of about the same magnitude. On top of that, the

European market for IT products and services which Eurogrid will by then have stimulated will amount to around $500 billion per annum —and be growing.

Although these may seem extraordinarily large numbers to the typical European lay observer, this will not be the case in the US or Japan, where the populace at large is generally alert to the great relevance of the IT sector to its economic success. This can be appreciated quite readily when it is recognised that the worldwide electronics/IT business is already the largest manufacturing sector of all: with global output currently approaching $2000 billion, it long ago outstripped vehicles and everything else. In Europe, on the other hand, our participation in this sparkling, high-growth, job-creating industrial activity has generally been so uneventful, so unproductive of either new jobs or noteworthy trade surpluses, that the public is largely unaware of the prosperity which can stem from the intelligent exploitation of electronics technology.

To illustrate, using the total production figure of $2000 billion quoted above, I estimate that global IT employment is currently around 8 million. Europe's share of the worldwide IT business has been hovering around a mere 10% for several years whereas, on the basis of its GDP or population, it should be closer to 25%. A simple calculation shows that if it had attained the level of 25%, Europe would have enjoyed the creation of about 1.2 million additional, primary, production jobs in electronics/IT alone, plus a consequent, substantial knock-on effect in secondary (supplier) sectors and in the other services, of course, which profit from the day-to-day spending of wage earners.

## Opportunities for all

The implications of Europe's endemic weakness in this sector are highly dispiriting. If the installation and operation of Eurogrid occurs after the current process of opening up the European telecommunications markets has been more or less completed, it will present tempting new opportunities for those foreign companies which have already mastered the commercial exploitation of the salient new technologies. In short, as things now stand, Europe's proposed new communications grid is less likely to provide the much-needed stimulation for European producers of its essential IT hardware, software and services than to represent a business bonanza for those non-European producers who have already travelled far along the learning curve.

Moreover, as stated, the skilled application of information technology is now fundamental to success in most areas of human endeavour, including financial activities, distribution and retailing, utilities, publishing, health care, agriculture and the extraction industries. In manufacturing, a wide variety of sectors now depend critically on IT to achieve world-class standards of product performance and cost — for example, vehicles, textiles, chemicals, metal forming, general engineering, instruments, food and general manufacturing. And it is well known that in many sectors good design has become so essential to competitive advantage, and so complex, that it can only be carried out effectively with the aid of sophisticated, computer-based systems.

In short, for 20 years at least, it has been clear to close observers of developments in IT that for many nations — whether newly or anciently industrialised — economic prosperity depends greatly on the degree to which, and the skills with which the nation understands and uses the currently most *avant garde* artefacts of the IT revolution. In this regard, America was the technological pioneer, applying electronics wizardry to the pursuit of military power, and Japan has grown rich by developing electronics goodies to serve mankind's innate desire for entertainment, comfort and convenience. Likewise, Singapore, Taiwan, South Korea and Hong Kong have shown how to compete with this trans-Pacific duopoly, especially when under the beneficial umbrella of an informed and supportive government. Europe, by contrast, is manifestly falling behind its less hidebound competitor nations and will slide further into an abyss of industrial and commercial incompetence unless and until it learns both to make and to use these essential modern tools.

Various policy initiatives to redress Europe's weaknesses in electronics/IT have been advocated for many years and have resulted, *inter alia,* in the Commission's major IT research and development (R&D) programmes such as ESPRIT, RACE and all the other acronymic roads to technological redemption. Unfortunately, although fairly successful within their own terms of reference, none of the massive, multi-billion Ecu projects has done much more than keep the European electronics industry afloat — just. It is a dismal fact that, outside the largely protected markets of defence and (to a decreasing extent) telecommunications, there is hardly a single, large, European-owned IT hardware producer which is, or has consistently been, profitable. Most of the largest players hang on because they see their involvement in electronics/IT as fundamental to their success in other manufacturing activities, or because they continue to hope that something will turn up, or because they simply do not know what else to do.

Thus, on the basis of the necessary improvements in communications, job creation and general competitiveness in manufacturing and commerce, there is a pressing need to address once again the basic causes of this European IT malaise, and to identify new policies for curing it. There can be no doubt that a renaissance strategy will be regarded as uncomfortably expensive by Europe's finance ministers and politically uncomfortable by those whose dedication to free and open markets transcends their commitment to the future economic well-being of Europe. Nevertheless, past policies having failed, in an increasingly vital industrial sector, there should be a great determination to generate new strategies which are concerned more and more with global competitiveness and less and less with political dogma. Above all else, there needs to be recognition in high places that it is only through capturing the technical high ground that Europe's chronic unemployment problem will begin to diminish.

**Boosting demand for IT**

A beginning can be made by recognising that the core of the problem lies in the relatively low use by Europeans of electronics and IT of all kinds. In the mid-1980s, for example, the *per capita* spend by Europeans on electronic goodies of all kinds (excluding only defence products) was less than half that of the United States. Moreover, despite — or perhaps because of — telephone tariffs which were generally much more expensive, the average European spent each year only about 45% as much on telecommunications services of all kinds as his American counterpart. And there is every reason to believe that things remain much the same today.

As to the reasons for this 'demand gap', one factor of great significance is the quality and intellectual predisposition of the European educational system. Too many European universities and institutions of higher education are still geared to the study of yesterday's classical or scientific verities rather than tomorrow's technological challenges. European students are generally less infused with the excitement of electronics than in America or Japan, with the result that, by international standards, they do not do very well at it — or do something else entirely. Recruitment into British science and engineering degree courses, for example, is falling, despite wide appreciation of the fact that a technical education confers greater vocational advantages.

The well-known predilections of the young to play with computer games or to misspend their youth among the paraphernalia of the computer shop, rather than the snooker hall, might be thought an encouraging sign for the future. But it is clearly not enough. The commercial exploitation of IT/electronics is not a game, but requires the highly disciplined application of a number of technical, innovatory, marketing and management skills, and it is evident that, in qualitative terms, at least, our educational institutions are not doing well enough.

Nor, indeed, in quantitative terms either. As one measure, the OECD recently reported that the annual output of third-level IT graduates in South Korea alone is about four times that of Britain and (then) West Germany put together. That statistic, if no other, should give us pause for thought in contemplating how to find ways out of Europe's economic and political malaise.

The anachronistic priorities and poor quality of many parts of Europe's higher educational system is to a large extent a self-perpetuating problem. With some exceptions, of course, today's teachers simply pass on their limitations and prejudices to the next generation, who do likewise, and it is extremely difficult to think of a means of breaking out of this slow spiral into technical oblivion. Perhaps firing an entire generation of university lecturers would do it, but that might meet with some opposition from vested interests in academe. Alternatively, we could provide financial inducements for inspired foreign technology teachers to ply their trade in Europe and for sending a proportion of our more promising students abroad for their higher technological education. One way or another, the *impasse* must be broken.

Parenthetically, there are those who argue that at the heart of all this is a cultural attitude which reflects nothing but credit on Europeans, who remain, by and large, and despite the world's headlong dash for technical nirvana, a civilized and stable people with secure social roots. I, at least, would not oppose such a view — but would add that it can only be by achieving world standards of technical competence and production levels that we shall be able to afford and enjoy the benefits of Europe's historical legacies.

Among the aspects of this problem which remain opaque to some of our policy makers, there is the salient matter of Europe's failure to invest in the means for actually producing these electronic 'all sorts'. After all, it is clear that, whatever the level of demand, or the state of our technology, IT jobs cannot be created if the captains of industry fail to build relevant factories. Indeed, government officials with responsibilities in the IT area are often frustrated by industry's timidity when faced with the need for high-tech investment. But it is not a straightforward matter.

A competent board of directors will obviously invest in production facilities only when it can see the prospect of a proper return — that is, when a market of sufficient size and quality exists (or is within sight) to take up the production at acceptable price levels. For this reason, if no other, Europe is not exactly short of car factories because, *inter alia,* the market is big and the existence of Orderly Marketing Agreements helps to stem the potential flood of technically superior Japanese cars.

In IT, however, the *per capita* market is relatively small and there is very little import protection apart from modest tariffs on some components, like micro-chips. Like cars, electronics is a global industry, based on the domination of economies of scale but, unlike cars, the pace of technical change in IT is extremely rapid, so if an IT company falls behind its fast-moving international competitors, it is in serious trouble. The costs of simply staying abreast of the leaders are nearly always daunting: trying at the same time to catch up can be financially devastating. The result is that the European IT industry, weakened by its errors of the past, is in poor shape to invest in its future.

In summary, to paint the picture as bleakly as it appears to those of us who have worried about such things for decades, Europe suffers from a relatively weak level of demand for IT/electronics products and this is exacerbated by a supplier industry which, cowed by its past mistakes, fails to invest adequately in the research, development, design and production activities which would enable us to lift ourselves by our bootstraps back into contention in global markets. What is to be done?

The answer lies in the self-same neural network with which this chapter began. But first it is useful to rehearse the reasoning which has led to these dispiriting conclusions:

> First, I have argued that the New Europe will not be viable — in either political, economic or administrative terms — without a new, efficient, pervasive and cheap telecommunications network.

> Second, other than for long-distance links, such a network as Eurogrid will not come about without support from the public purse because there is simply not enough in it for Europe's PTOs, many of whom are moving — albeit hesitantly — towards a privatised future. (Meanwhile, they are distracted by the transient attractions of the so-called Integrated Services Digital Network, despite its huge limitations in relation to Eurogrid.)

> Third, even if the rate of installation of Eurogrid were to accelerate, the weakness of European IT producers is such that, in the absence of other measures, the stimulated demand for the electronic widgets which will go into the new network will largely be met by non-European suppliers, whose commitment to the future economic well-being of Europe might be supposed to somewhat lacking.

## Broadband investment

Thus the way ahead is now clear. Predicated on the belief, already stated, that the economic future of the New Europe depends on a pervasive, highly efficient and low-cost pan-European communications network, backed up by an internationally competitive IT/electronics industry, itself serving to sustain global competitiveness in a host of user sectors, the following policy decisions need to be taken with some speed.

In the first place, EC governments and the Commission must redirect the bulk of their considerable IT support budgets away from research and development programmes and towards demand-stimulation activities. The only one of these large enough to have sufficient economic effect is Eurogrid, although a host of subsidiary projects could also accelerate the much-needed boost to Europe's competitiveness in industry and commerce.

Priority in these re-focused efforts should be given to the rapid completion of the complex but excruciatingly drawn-out discussions about establishing pan-European standards for operation of the network — the communication protocols, network frequencies, terminal specifications and so forth. There is already some momentum towards this goal, largely through the medium of the Commission's programme on Research on Advanced Communications in Europe (RACE), but these deliberations need a much greater sense of urgency.

Running a close second should be the creation of financial incentives for the PTOs to accelerate the installation of local-loop, broadband connections to both business and domestic premises. One significant incentive in the UK and, by implication, elsewhere would be permission for the PTOs to carry entertainment traffic, notably TV, on Eurogrid in addition to the conventional and newer forms of voice and data communications which they would in any event expect to carry. (Parenthetically, it is typical of official myopia about such matters that, in the UK, it is expected that British Telecom will have to wait several years before being granted — if ever — such rights to carry entertainment traffic.)

This pan-European policy initiative for broadband communications should be reinforced by encouraging more competitors into the local-loop business, including operators offering alternative connection technologies such as narrowband radio fusion (or wireless) with or without a cellular/mobile dimension. By this means, and over a period of 20 years, Europe should be fitted out with the kind of communications infrastructure which would carry it efficiently through most of the next century.

To those who worry about how such a broadband network would be used, or would generate the traffic to make it financially viable, it is only necessary to point to the extraordinary and unpredictable advances which electronics has made over the past 40 years and its huge growth in economic importance. Given a network with the postulated low tariffs and high capabilities, traders, policemen, musicians, developers, television producers, journalists, photographers, researchers, advertisers, artists, estate agents, scientists, doctors, stock brokers, newspapers, architects, entertainers (hopefully of not too dubious a nature), accountants, travel agents, retailers, bankers, farmers, librarians, wholesalers, manufacturers and entrepreneurs generally will flock to use the network to meet their own specific needs. New enterprises will spring up to offer new services totally unknown today, and it can confidently be expected that man's innovative talents will serve to fill all available parts of Eurogrid's very broad frequency spectrum.

In like manner, distributed computing — now emerging unequivocally as the preferred alternative to big, centralised mainframes — will be given a powerful boost, as will new trans-frontier, multi-media, E-mail and data-interchange techniques such as EDI, referred to earlier. All of this, needless to say, will be to the enhanced competitive advantage of the enterprises which embrace these efficient new communication systems.

**Facing up to the competition**

Running in parallel with this long-term strategic investment in communications, the New Europe must grasp the nettle of providing some temporary protection for its nascent IT producers. As already pointed out, an important part of the justification for Eurogrid is the demand stimulation it will provide for a wide variety of IT terminals. It is imperative that this enhanced market is used to give the European IT producers an opportunity — possibly their last! — to invest themselves back into international contention. Given a selective shield from the full force of unbridled international competition, plus some help in easing their over-stretched balance sheets, these companies should have all the incentives they need to put their technologies — generally adequate enough for the task ahead — to work in the creation of new sales of new products in new markets. All this will result in many new jobs.

For the fact is that the IT industry needs Europe as much as Europe needs Eurogrid. As already stated, the industry is largely based on the exploitation of substantial economies of scale, stemming mainly from the incredible mass-production capabilities of the micro-chip. Thus IT needs large markets for standardised products and, in the case of European suppliers,

Europe is the best and nearest. Provided robust steps are taken to ensure real competition between European producers, giving them some preferential access to the enormous new market which Eurogrid will create will represent a unique opportunity for them to ramp up their sales and production levels to global standards. If, after all that, they still cannot compete when the veil of protection is removed in 20 years time, Europe can really kiss good-bye to any prospects of achieving prosperity through the production of information technology artefacts.

But such a gloomy outcome is quite unrealistic. Nobody claims that European technology is generally inferior to that of our international competitors: nor is it feasible to postulate that some genetic, cultural or ethnic characteristic makes us incapable of creating successful high-technology industries (look, for example, at the British pharmaceutical sector, the French commitment to Airbus Industrie, or the German chemicals producers). It is simply the fact that, in a period when the global electronics industry experienced unprecedented change and growth, most large European producers were badly placed — for a variety of reasons — to exploit these expanding markets. To miss the boat in this business, is to fall into a shark-infested ocean.

What cannot be overlooked, of course, is the international furore which would be occasioned by a 'Shield Europe' policy, even when confined to selected parts of the IT sector and to a limited number of years. Europe's US and Far Eastern competitors are too aware of the future importance of this sector not to make a determined fight to maintain their current domination of the European IT market. But they will need to be persuaded through concessions in other areas (the Common Agricultural Policy comes to mind). In any event, Europe is too big to be pushed around easily. The outcome of such external pressures will turn on the appreciation by Europe's governments of the salience of the IT sector to Europe's economic future, and their courage in resisting these pressures.

## Europe's IT renaissance

Through the establishment of Eurogrid and the gradual renaissance of the European IT industry, the remaining problems will decay gently into insignificance. The ineffectiveness of the educational sector will wither in the face of an upsurge of technical knowhow generally and in higher education particularly. Financial institutions, recognising a good thing when they see it, will eschew short-termism and go for a tempting piece of the long-term action. Governments will preside over a gradual reduction in their social security burdens as unemployment falls to the more acceptable levels of the 1970s. Information Technology users, recognising a confident new climate favouring the intelligent application of IT tools, will invest in products and services to make themselves globally competitive. And the European IT industry itself will recover confidence in its ability to profit from technology and will establish the basic technical, financial and managerial strengths to enable it to ride future waves of technological change.

In summary, the 'neural' network, Eurogrid, will eventually both drive, and be driven by, the power of the European vision. It is already justifiable in both economic and political terms. The renaissance of the European IT industry goes hand-in-hand with Eurogrid as an essential contribution to the preservation of Europe as a prosperous, high-employment, big-time player in the global high-tech markets of the third millennium. Failure to do these things will result in Europe becoming merely a collection of Once-Industrialised Countries — or OICs. We need to start now.

---

[1]  Ian Mackintosh *Sunrise Europe*, Oxford: Basil Blackwell, 1986.

# Chapter Six

# Building Europe's Infrastructure

## Keith Richardson

The complex subject of European infrastructure has three separate claims on our interest: it is of vast economic importance, it was the defining issue that marked the serious entry of business onto the European policy-making stage, and it provides a paradigm example of the potential that the European approach can offer if we can learn how to manage it properly.

It is a curious paradox that business was so little involved in the Community's early years. Admittedly, the fundamental driving force lay more on the political side, with the burning desire to avoid the repetition of wars which had brought the humiliating experiences of defeat and occupation to virtually every nation of continental Europe — a factor which still continues to explain the different emotional attitudes towards Europe between the British and their partners.

Yet although the machinery of the Community and the main thrust of its activity was largely economic, business was still kept at arm's length. Jean Monnet was quite open about this. He regarded the big companies as too nationalistic in their outlook. The concepts of social democracy and the international ideals of the trade union movement seemed the more natural partners (another legacy which lingers on today). The rolling waves of economic progress were what mattered, and set against this vision the businessmen were something of a nuisance factor, like the stinging jellyfish that mar a summer holiday.

By the early 1980s the failure of this approach was evident. The European system as founded by Monnet was not performing well. Euro-sclerosis was in vogue. The big companies whose horizons had spread to envelop the global economy could clearly see the unsatisfactory state of their own backyard. Businessmen began to share the blame for the fact that the Community's handling of economic questions was inadequate. Strongly organised though they were in their various national federations, they were failing to provide an adequate input into policy-making at European level.

This perception was shared by the Commission itself, which, trying to break out of the old straitjacket, was heard to complain '... if we want to talk to European industry, who do we ring up?'.

## Business wakes up

Two responses came more or less simultaneously. The national industrial federations overhauled and strengthened their European confederation UNICE, as the official voice of business, while the leaders of some of the big companies established the European Round Table of Industrialists (ERT) as a policy group of senior chairmen and chief executives. Private and unofficial, the ERT acts as a complement to UNICE. The two bodies liaise closely and to some extent divide responsibilities between them. Right from the start it was the ERT that made the running on the subject of infrastructure polices, and a direct line can be traced from the ERT's widely read first policy report *Missing Links*, published in 1984, to the formal commitment on Trans-European Networks enshrined in the Maastricht Treaty. The words are there, the arguments are well marshalled and widely accepted. But after a decade of pressure the practical results still fall sadly short.

The central concept which drives the infrastructure issue in the eyes of business is that of international competitiveness. It is, first of all, a supply-side problem. Today, no doubt everyone is aware that international trade has been the motor of worldwide economic growth for more than a generation. Protectionism is as outmoded a concept as the planned economy. Companies have learned the hard way that if they cannot compete on the world stage they cannot survive at home. Incompetent businessmen have been wiped out by foreign competitors whose names they cannot pronounce and whose home base they cannot even find on a map.

However, view this bracing environment through the eyes of business people. They have to compete worldwide, and of course the first responsibility rests on them and their colleagues alone. Yet the pressure for ever-greater efforts and ingenuity is unceasing. So, the argument goes, if my export efforts are not to be wasted then my home base must also be at least as well organised as those of my competitors. European business people tend to believe that the American and Asian environments are more favourable to the development of competitive businesses than the European. From this perception stems the insistent demand that Europe needs a much better infrastructure if it is to prosper.

The concept of 'infrastructure' can of course be applied widely, and it is perfectly proper to speak of legal, financial or scientific infrastructure. The argument is much the same in each case. But here let us focus on the paradigm case which is transport infrastructure, the easiest to define and the one most obviously the victim of geographical antiquarianism.

Return to our business people. If our competitors, they may argue, are based in a country such as the US or Japan which has one single transport system — one single and integrated road, rail or air network — they have a tremendous advantage. They can move people, goods and services more cheaply than us. What is more, they are ahead of us in terms of speed, reliability and flexibility — and these are the three factors which, even more than costs, really determine competitiveness in the modern business environment.

In contrast, what do we have here in Europe? A fragmented hotch-potch of antiquated systems built to service nation states whose economic relevance has long since departed. We try to treat the Community as a single market and a single base for our operations, but that means dealing not with six transport networks as in Jean Monnet's day, but with twelve, or with twenty including EFTA or thirty as we are drawn further into Central and Eastern Europe. Such an accumulation of inefficiencies puts a burden on the back of everyone who works in European industry.

So much for the general argument, which has to be restated in the simplest possible terms, because regular contact with government reveals that they have great difficulty in understanding any of it. It is easy to see why.

Governments in most countries play the dominant role in infrastructure investment. On the whole they spend money in response to political pressures which by their very nature are set in local terms. A bypass, a rail link, a new airport 'for my town', or alternatively 'over my dead body' — these are the terms of political debate. The deciding voice is that of local electorates. Considerable pressure is exerted by employees, which inevitably shifts the balance to the more inefficient systems because they have the most jobs at stake. The interests of international businessmen (many of whom live in foreign countries and cast their votes elsewhere) are hardly a relevant factor. To overcome such hostility and inertia the business community has had to develop the argument in considerable detail. It is possible here only to highlight some of the main points before considering how they impact on the central issue of European decision-making.

## The economic need

The starting point is to see infrastructure as an economic input, and on this basis to identify a system that can deliver the best quality at the lowest cost. The role of business should be clear. Individual companies may be suppliers of infrastructure, and very properly each will try to market their own systems as best they can. But industry as a whole is a user of infrastructure, and that is where the public interest lies.

Concern about European competitiveness is today at a peak. Since 1980 there has been an almost continuous decline in the Community's market share of world exports measured by volume. One direct consequence is rising unemployment, about which governments seem so much at a loss. Of all the factors affecting competitiveness, the one which governments are best placed to do something about at relatively short notice is infrastructure. The Round Table sent this message to the Birmingham and Edinburgh European Councils in 1992. It certainly received a degree of response in terms of additional investment finance — but no real change in procedures.

## The European dimension

Here lies the crucial difference between the Monnet era and the 1990s. Today industry treats Europe as one market, with its operations highly integrated. One advantage of Europe is that there are many people and resources within a small area. But that advantage is offset by the natural and inevitable corollary of congestion. It is then made much worse by the additional and unnecessary burden of fragmentation. Fragmentation is what lay behind the original concept of *Missing Links* — the attempt to define those links between countries, across the Alps, the Baltic or the Channel, for example, which were of greater importance to Europe as a whole than to the individual countries.

Today industry would generalise the concept and argue that the infrastructure problems can only be solved at European level. Our economic future is entirely in the hands of those businesses that trade and invest across frontiers. States working on their own are helpless to solve their problems. The French High Speed Train was perhaps the last of the great 'one-nation' initiatives, whose benefits are only slowly assuming a European dimension, but generations far into the future will change trains at Cologne and wonder why we did not devise one single system for the continent instead of two.

## Technology

The purely technical constraints seem relatively few in number. The High Speed Train and the Channel Tunnel both demonstrate the ability to overcome substantial technical problems. But to solve technical problems requires more than purely technical skills. It needs some degree of certainty about the future market — one of the secrets behind the High Speed Train's success. It needs some certainty about regulatory controls — unnecessary changes in which have seriously delayed the Channel Tunnel. It needs a commitment to integration — the development of combined road-rail systems, for example, crucially depends on having the same handling equipment at every interchange system from Manchester to Milan. It also needs a willingness to suppress local private empires — which constitute the main barrier to the integration of air traffic control in Europe.

### Networks and systems

These considerations lead naturally to the notion of Trans-European networks, designed to serve the needs of Europe as a whole. Let us be clear. Networking does not mean single ownership or single management. But it does require some form of integrated planning to realise the benefits of integrated movement without trans-shipment, the inter-operability of hardware, the simplification of administrative procedures and the validity of cost comparisons.

The basic concept is no different from the way in which industry plans an oil refinery, a chemical plant or a new aircraft, where innumerable different inputs flow along different channels to yield many different but consistent outputs. There are well-established methods to plan such a system as a whole, to optimise its performance, and to quantify the gains resulting from new investment, while still decentralising the care of each element to its own on-the-spot management.

Systems engineering is today a discipline in its own right which teaches operators to think firstly of the ultimate results, in terms of overall flows of people or products from A to B, and only secondly of the bits of hardware involved. One lesson which emerges clearly is that the performance of hardware can be radically improved if information is readily available about what is happening elsewhere in the system — where is congestion building up, where have accidents blocked the normal flows, where is spare capacity available? One of the major benefits to come from the systems approach to Trans-European Networks should lie in the development of integrated information systems designed to do exactly that. An aircraft circling over its destination, a car driving towards a traffic jam or a lorry making a return journey empty — they are all wasting time and fuel and yet they reflect a failure of information far more than a failure of basic hardware.

## The problem of choice

From Roman roads onwards, the infrastructure we use today was largely designed for other needs, essentially for a differently shaped Europe. The network approach imposes a natural requirement to think through the needs of today and to assess tomorrow's needs too, as far as we can judge them. An overall reappraisal would cast much light on such apparent weaknesses in the current system as the inadequacy of East-West corridors in Europe as compared to North-South, the persistent under-utilisation of railways for freight transport or the extraordinary neglect of maritime transport at a time when so many great ports are half empty.

Not that anybody suggests some wild idea of rebuilding everything. But systems engineering on a European level would be well placed to indicate where to put investment to bring the maximum benefit to the network as a whole. Value for money is an essential concept here, and some of the main priorities can be tentatively identified:

> • Congestion-free links between the main industrial and commercial centres: London to Paris, southern Germany to northern Italy, Antwerp to the Ruhr, Lyons to Turin and Barcelona. Costs are high, but so are the benefits, and so is the potential for information systems that can make the best use of the limited space available.

> • Long-distance links bringing peripheral regions like Ireland, Greece or Portugal into closer contact with the economic mainstream. In these cases, where distances are greater and traffic flows are lighter, the correct solutions will be quite different from in the central regions. But the whole European economy benefits if outlying regions can be helped to generate their own economic growth and to cure their own unemployment instead of exporting it.

> • Public transport systems to cure urban congestion. When many large cities are becoming both unlivable and unmanageable, this counts as a European as well as a local problem. The speed and reliability of long-distance transport are restricted by local congestion, both at terminal points and at cities that have to be navigated *en route*. The costs of production and employment as

well as of transport and communications are damaged by the inefficiency of cities, which are where most company headquarters are located. These factors will critically affect future decisions on the location of new industries and the development of the new Europe's principal business centres.

• 'Debottlenecking' — a long word for the simple process of bringing existing systems to their full potential. It is, for example, pure nonsense to build a Channel Tunnel and then refuse to give it proper rail links at both ends. Conversely the direct benefit to be gained from even now building such links to London and beyond would be substantial and would add to the rewards for having built the Tunnel in the first place. Much the same applies to air transport, where a higher return comes from balancing air space and ground facilities than from investing merely in one or the other.

## Finance

Enough has been said to show that the underlying need for new investment in infrastructure is high, even allowing for the greater efficiency of a systems approach. Yet the actual level of investment has declined from 1.5% to 0.9% of GDP over the last 20 years, reckoning surface transport only. Such a decline — 30 billion Ecu a year in current terms — cannot possibly be related to true needs. It rather reflects the role of governments who are increasingly short of money and see infrastructure as an area for apparently painless expenditure cuts, since their accounting makes no reckoning of the wider economic benefits which are thus foregone.

Needless to say, it would be of little value to suggest that governments should simply spend more money, even if they were in a position to do so. That is not how benefits are maximised. What is needed is to match supply to effective economic demand and this can only be done by bringing the mechanism of the market more fully into play. The essential concept to emerge from the European Round Table's recent studies is that the user should pay. The user should pay directly for the benefit received and the services exploited, and should not contribute through the tax system to a general pool of infrastructure which everyone then uses free of charge.

Payment by the user gives a direct measure of economic benefit. But it also opens the way for the more effective use of private finance and private management of transport systems. If the benefit is greater than the costs, and if the benefit is turned into hard cash at the point of use through the 'user-pays' principle, then in theory we have a perfect scenario for risk capital financed privately in the expectation of profit. Reality will not often match that scenario entirely. Most infrastructure projects have a wider impact that cannot be ignored. There will be political constraints and uncertainties outside the control of the businessmen, especially where the pay-back period is measured in decades not years. But such factors can be quantified, however roughly, and assigned a cash value.

The standard model for the future would be one in which governments normally put up a minority share of finance to cover their own interests, with the private sector providing the rest and managing it as efficiently as possible to produce its own reward. Industry and government should certainly not try to take over each other's responsibilities; the idea is rather that of partnership to ensure that resources are combined to meet genuine economic needs. Of course governments will continue to share in the decisions about infrastructure — it could hardly be otherwise — but the influence of the market on the decisions would become greater as a result of the normal process of investors assessing risks and rewards.

**The social interest**

If this analysis has focused on the hard economics of infrastructure policies, and called for a rigorous measurement of costs and benefits through the market system, this is not to ignore the wider interests at play. Indeed the whole purpose is to enable the mobilisation of greater resources which can also be used to meet other demands and so serve those wider interests. A few examples will show the potential.

* The individual can turn his own purchasing power into a bigger car today, but not into a faster road, which might be more useful to him. If new toll-roads were built to reflect economic needs then he would have a choice, to use them and pay or not, which is unavailable to him today.

* The local community has strong environmental priorities, which are often difficult to realise. It is much easier to prevent new developments than to make them happen. Yet a great deal of environmental damage can be directly attributed to the survival of out-of-date and inadequate infrastructure, designed in other times to meet other needs. It is by building new transport systems that city centres can be liberated, not by forcing people on to old systems or even trying to stop movement altogether.

* Wider political objectives can also properly be brought into play. One relevant example is the integration of Central and Eastern Europe. It is arguable that more progress would have been made if that region's overall infrastructure needs had been analysed at the outset in terms of transnational systems and networks, and financial backing then found.

## New approach to policy-making

Enough has been said to indicate the potential of a new approach to infrastructure in Europe, an approach that is at the same time more coherent and more market driven. Mobility across the continent would be seen as a general benefit. Users would pay for what they used. Entrepreneurs would invest in what they judged to be profitable opportunities. Governments would pay not for the whole system but for a portion to match their own political priorities.

To bring these ideas to fruition there is no fundamental problem of finance, technology or information, all of which can readily be procured. The real challenge rests with the ability of government to make the plans and take the decisions. The issues are complex — but so are many of the issues that plague modern Europe. Indeed, infrastructure poses in a very precise way the geographical problem of reconciling all the dimensions involved: trans-continental, national, regional and local. None of these can be ignored. Here is a central problem of European politics. Is it possible that by examining how governments might address this somewhat practical and even prosaic topic we might cast light on wider questions?

Since we began by emphasising infrastructure as an economic input, with a critical impact on business performance, it might be useful to take the analysis in two stages, treating it first as a management problem and then in a wider political context. At first sight the issue presents itself in simple terms of centralisation versus decentralisation, on which businessmen have a good deal to say. But their view of power structures is not necessarily the same as the political view. Within a company power flows in different ways. Ultimate control normally flows down from the top, expressed as legal authority, the right to hire and fire, the grip on the purse strings. But another power flows from the bottom upwards, the power of customers and employees, without whom the business is worthless.

Long experience has shown that pyramid power structures cannot deal with this reality. A chairman can give orders, but if his employees do not produce products that customers want to buy all is in vain. It is the operational managers who are closest to customers and employees and determine the real success of the business, and modern management systems are designed to give such managers the maximum degree of responsibility. But the centre still determines the strategic direction and sets the guidelines within which the managers must work and by which they are judged. It is a common judgement that it is only when everybody is fully agreed on the overall direction that control can be loosed and decentralisation yield its full potential.

Now apply this concept to infrastructure. Imagine some experienced industrial manager given the job of rebuilding Europe's infrastructure. One thing that is clear is that he would not assemble a hundred thousand officials into one centre, in Brussels or elsewhere, to manage it all from the top downwards. One might more readily expect (1) an executive board to determine the main lines of development and allocate the central resources; (2) a strategic planning team to evaluate networks as a whole, especially the links between different transport modes, and to establish a valid basis for comparing costs and benefits; and (3) a relatively tight financial control and audit team to measure performance. Such a manager would inevitably want to decentralise operational management. The only open question is whether he would design the second tier on geographical lines (UK infrastructure as a single unit) or in modal terms (European railways under one control). Either way could be made to work and over time they would no doubt both be tried. But the duties of local managers would be clearly defined: to develop infrastructure systems that reflected the overall strategy, fitted in with local needs, and yielded good value for money.

## Decentralisation

The political view of decentralisation does not run on quite the same lines. In fact the word means different things to different people — a factor which largely accounts for the general confusion in Europe about 'federalism'.[1] In France power flows downwards, in Switzerland it flows upwards, in Germany it is distributed according to a precise legal text, in the US it flows along contradictory paths, and in the UK it is centralised as nowhere else.

In the European Community the power structure is almost exactly the opposite of the business model. Ultimate control rests clearly with the operating units — the member states. Main administrative action lies at the centre — and it is the centre that the customer — or the voter — sees. The Commission makes proposals, as officials are trained to do, the Council of Ministers haggles towards decisions, which the Commission then tries to apply, but nobody is in strategic control of any policy area at all. Hence many evils. Put crudely, within the European system there is nobody who can be fired when anything goes wrong. The buck stops nowhere.

A more rational approach to European infrastructure policies would require political control at the highest level. Those who carried political responsibility would listen to all the conflicting advice and pressures and then take decisions, for which they would answer directly to the electors. These decisions would become framework plans for air traffic control, for inland waterways, for urban transport. A general plan would allow different modes of transport to compete on equal terms and to cooperate without difficulty, while a financial structure opened the way for user charges and private investment. Independent sources of advice would be of great value, such as the proposed European Centre for Infrastructure Studies which the ERT is currently helping to promote.

Implementation would rest largely with entrepreneurs. Technical standardisation would be worked out by specialists working within the framework. Access to land would require a local political input which would carry great weight but not amount to a right of veto. Plans which met a trans-European need would benefit from preferential access to long-term finance. Plans meeting purely local needs would depend on local finance. And the impact of such works on the total European economic and financial system would certainly call for regular review and occasional changes of gear laid down from the centre.

## Institutional reform

The implications are substantial. But this radical debate should not be ideological. The argument is simply that structures should follow needs. The un-met needs of today are largely European in scale, so what is described is essentially a European decision-making structure. What exactly should be the nature of that structure, and how to get there from here, are highly political questions. But if one is thinking of personal not collective responsibility, of control by elected politicians rather than by appointed officials, of national plans fitting into a European framework rather than coming together on an ad hoc basis, then one is certainly looking at something rather different from the way in which things are done today. It is not to be achieved by mimicking national structures. Nobody wants to create European super-ministries. Still less is it to be achieved by drawing legal demarcation lines between national and European administrations, as though they were not supposed to be serving a single common good. What is needed is a synergy between what is done at the European level and what is done nationally, not the institutionalised conflict which seems latent in that seductive notion of subsidiarity.

In the end it is a question of political will. If Europeans want to be competitive we will have to cooperate far more closely on those issues that fundamentally determine competitiveness, such as infrastructure. A national approach will not work. An adequate approach at European level cannot be provided by the present system. A new system of managing that European level will therefore be needed and that should be one of the clear objectives of the 1996 Intergovernmental Conference. It is hopeless to pretend that change can be avoided. The search will be difficult. No doubt some characteristically devious European compromise will emerge, but the search will be helped if we can establish some criteria for judging the EC institutions in the field of transport policy and infrastructure development:

- they should be capable of setting a strategic direction to handle those problems that are of European significance;

- they should fulfil the tasks of overall management;

- they should communicate with the electorate, explain, win support or accept responsibility for failure;

- they should balance one policy, such as infrastructure, with other priorities such as regional planning and macroeconomic management;

- they should be under political control and be light on central bureaucracy;

- they should make maximum use of market mechanisms, decentralise all management within the agreed strategic framework, and show maximum respect for local diversity.

These are the objectives, and this is where the debate should start.

---

[1] For a fuller discussion of these issues, see Andrew Duff ed. *Subsidiarity Within the European Community*, London: The Federal Trust, 1993.

Chapter Seven

# A New Model of Environmental Development

## Andrew Warren

This chapter seeks to expand on one aspect, environmental policy, of the basic diagnosis of EC Commission President Jacques Delors of the present economic and employment crisis facing Western Europe. In that environment policy reaches across all sectors of the economy, it is clearly a vital element in any recovery strategy.[1]

My predominant thesis is that the present crisis does not simply follow those recurrent within the established economic cycle. This crisis is far more structural and all-embracing, touching practically every aspect of our society. It would be no exaggeration to describe it as being simultaneously environmental, technological, educational, urban, social and moral. Of particular concern is the way various environmental problems have both multiplied and for the most part worsened in recent years — culminating in the threat which climate change poses to our very existence as a society. This, together with other profound changes that have been occurring in every other facet of our society, have come to a head under the impact of the acute economic crisis.

### The European urban system

Of particular concern are the pressures currently being placed upon the cities of Europe themselves. They can safely be described as currently passing through one of their worst periods. Most of these cities were created as a consequence of the pressure to seek external economies and scale economies, both perceived as essential to the growth of industrial society. Given the subsequent transformations of industry and employment, many of these cities have now outlived their economic purpose, and are becoming obsolete for the service and information oriented societies of today. Swiftly degenerating urban areas are responsible for at least 80% of all the damage inflicted upon the environment with considerable cost to the economy — and for a large percentage, for the high criminality and anti-social behaviour of their inhabitants.

If we designed our new urban areas to fit the new economic and social reality we could achieve an altogether more positive picture. In practice, much of the current economic trends could assist this change. There is an increasing need for greater flexibility in centres of economic activity. Much contemporary industry is far less obnoxious than the old smokestack industries as far as the environment is concerned. Increasing dependence upon communication technologies for so much social intercourse means that we could do away with the dichotomy of the distances between where people live and where they work.

This would help to reduce industrial concentrations and high density developments, and simultaneously dramatically minimise transport movements for work purposes — of itself, of substantial environmental benefit. Redesigning our urban areas would create far more humanly manageable areas, with a salutary influence upon their inhabitants. It would also create a lot of employment.

To stop the flight to the ever-expanding suburbs, and the further depopulation and spoilation of our inner cities, Europe needs dynamic municipal government to drive through imaginative policies. Glasgow's recent concentration on the arts and Sheffield's on sport are two good examples of urban refurbishment. Hi-tech investment is clearly attracted to towns with a quality educational base and a pleasant environment, such as Cambridge. There is considerable scope to attract cultural and environmental sponsorship for civic improvements from in-coming companies. The need for social housing in the inner cities is also intense, but this, too, requires local government to forsake its traditionally bureaucratic and hierarchical ways. In the best European cities, conservation is now regarded as an important element of community politics. Local and regional government are often at the leading edge of environmental policy.

### Attitudes to the environment

We have traditionally treated the environment as an expendable valueless commodity. The final and painful realisation of this profligacy comes now that we have reached a point where our lives — and more importantly, the lives of our children — are at risk. The root cause seems to be the basic misconception of treating the environment as if it is a cost—free element, to be sacrificed on the altar of economic growth. In practice, natural resources are no different to raw materials, and should be valued similarly. Whether we have zero growth or substantial growth, we are heading towards an environmental catastrophe if that growth is not genuinely sustainable. Despite serious — and sometimes expensive — environmental legislation from both the European Community and many of its member states independently, and despite increasing awareness throughout all member states of environmental problems, the state of the environment continues to deteriorate. And at the same time, the population of the world continues to grow substantially, with increasing demands from that new population for material wealth along European lines.

The moral and social crisis which characterises our societies is undeniably associated with the failure of our urban systems, with the social evil of persistent large scale unemployment, but also with a more general breakdown in our system of cultural, moral, and religious values. No single one of these changes is by itself culpable. No single one by itself is reprehensible. However, the cocktail, as currently blended, is wholly indigestible.

**The environment in harmony with the economy**

Firstly, is there a possible solution? What is needed is a new development model, based upon the integration of the environment into our economic thinking, as opposed to the traditional — and sterile — antithesis of placing environmental issues versus economic growth. Such a new approach would constitute a radical solution to the problem of development and quality of life. It does so by making the environment one of the new locomotives for healthier growth.

How can this be done? Before answering this question we have to distinguish between two roles played by environmental action, which, of themselves, generate economic activity and employment. The first may be called the 'protective' role. This is the more familiar environmental role. It consists of the efforts to save or restore our environment mainly through legislating environmental standards, and then enforcing them. Some examples of this are, for instance, sewage treatment, and the industries which produce the infrastructural equipment for it; building codes and the industries which support these; 'cleaner' cars and the new technology associated with them.

The second role can be defined as the 'active' role. This is when action for the environment directly increases the competitiveness of our products and thus our economies. Two good examples are the reduction of costs brought about by environmental packaging, which may in some cases halve the cost of packaging, via re-use or recycling; or by energy saving measures in commerce and industry which lead to considerable reductions in overheads on expenditure upon fuels. However, the importance of taking integrated action on an EC or pan-European basis is incontrovertible: the new German packaging regulations threaten to impede the Single Market.

The difference between the two roles is that the protective role certainly creates additional economic activity and plenty of jobs, but — at least in the short run — adds to the cost of operating our economies under existing market conditions. It therefore incorporates the risk of pricing ourselves out of certain world markets. It was the fear of such economic consequences which led to the intensive orchestration of antipathy to the proposed EC energy/carbon tax from the larger industrial companies within the Community.

However, the active role presents an immediate net gain both for the competitiveness of our economies and also has substantial job creation potential in both the short run and the medium term. Of course, in real life the two roles are not always separate. The higher standards for better buildings, for instance, incorporating more energy saving devices, do, in the short run, add to the costs both of housing and commercial building construction (although not to their operation). Fairly soon, however, the development of these technologies, triggered by such activities, leads to the creation of even more efficient buildings with considerably lower fuel consumption.

Even the EC carbon/energy tax, which is aimed to stabilize emissions at 1990 levels by the year 2000, would serve to reduce costs by increasing energy efficiency. The rate proposed by the Commission is to add $10 per barrel of oil equivalent. Opposition to the proposal comes mainly from the UK and the poorer countries of the EC on grounds (mainly) of cost, and from France, who wishes to exempt its nuclear energy. It is clearly not yet accepted by EC member governments that environmental action is not only inherently good, but that it sharpens industry's competitive edge and can create many new jobs. Jacques Delors has a task in his White Paper to persuade. His colleague, Commissioner Paleokrassas estimates that an EC-wide plan for energy-saving in housing could yield 35 million job-years.[2]

### New environmental development model

To return now to the original question: assuming that in the long run both environmental roles — protective and active — are agreed to be of net benefit, how do we alter the present highly unsatisfactory economic and environmental position to obtain this new environmental model? How do we get from here to there?

There should be a four part approach:

First, there is an urgent need for an in-depth research programme into the full economic implications of environmental action. The objective must be to enable us to assess accurately the various costs and benefits in terms of growth, employment and technology advancement, both in the short and long term, of all of the options. This should be undertaken in conjunction with the following proposal.

Second, a revolutionary orientation of both our accounting and tax systems. The latter would shift from the present basis of taxing labour and profits to a new pollution and resource basis, including land-use taxes. 'Green accounting' and 'green taxation' represent the most practical and efficient way of incorporating the environment into our economy.

Third, the complete removal of any economical barriers which are established to deter environmental action — for example, the taxation of energy-saving items at a higher rate than energy consumption — and any other such barriers revealed by the proposed research programme.

Fourth, a long-term plan should be undertaken regarding the best models for urban and rural developments, and the best methods to integrate our existing historical city centres into them.

In adopting this approach, it is possible that a number of unexpected consequences may ensue. Some may even in the short term cause substantial difficulties. However, even at this stage, what cannot be disputed is the requirement for a new, global approach to the interconnected questions of sustainable growth and employment, and the general integration of the environment into our economic and social thinking.

The new overall philosophy must address not only the problems of revitalising ageing economies without damaging the environment, but also produce a new model for healthy urban and rural areas. In addition, it could help us to solve those elements of the social and moral crisis which are connected directly with these problems.

In summary, what is required is a taxation system based upon the use of resources. This must encourage an automatic reduction in volumes of waste, as well as the removal of bottlenecks within the system which fail to increase the overall efficiency of the re-use, recycle and waste disposal cycle.

Other economic and financial instruments should be explored, such as a system of marketable pollution rights, or a comprehensive and correctly priced system of permits covering the environmental costs. The overall objective is intended to move towards a 'resource-oriented' fiscal system. This represents a radical departure from our present tax system which (albeit accidentally) deliberately penalises labour and production, and directly encourages the profligate use of resources.

It is not possible at this stage to define what exactly the true cost of each form of pollution is. A lengthy joint study between the EC and the United States Department of Energy is endeavouring to take some of the initial steps along this route. Nonetheless, it has to be accepted that it is difficult enough setting the right surrogate figures to cover such 'unfriendly' emissions as sulphur and carbon dioxide let alone factoring in other issues like noise and land-use policy. The long-term safety and economic viability of nuclear energy remains deeply controversial.

However, the cardinal rule behind the Community's environmental policy for the future has to be that there is one financial figure which is known, and known to be wrong: that is the present policy of charging the environmental despoliation at zero cost. What is required in the Delors recovery programme — and more pertinently in its implementation — are a series of sea-changes in the way in which this issue is approached by EC member governments. It is quite impossible for any one national economy — however large — to take such steps in isolation. That is why the European Community, as the world's largest integrated trading block, has a particular responsibility in moving this concept forward. That is not to suggest that any such steps will be easy.

Nicolo Machiavelli epitomised well the problem before us:— "There is nothing more difficult than to initiate a new order of things. For the reformer has enemies in all who profit by the old order, and only lukewarm defenders in all those who would profit by the new order".

Nonetheless, if the Community is to have any role relating to the environment it must be to embrace these radical changes in the remaining years left in this millennium.

---

[1] Although the UK government's contribution to the Delors debate makes no mention of environment policy at all. See HM Treasury & Department of Employment *Growth, Competitiveness & Employment in the European Community*, London, 30 July 1993.
[2] Financial Times, 28 October 1993.

Chapter Eight

# Towards More Flexible Labour Markets

David Goodhart

When a Spanish businessman has a profitable year he does not invest in plant and equipment to expand his business and create jobs. Instead he puts money aside to cover the large cost of sacking workers when the market turns down. Felipe Gonzalez, Spain's Prime Minister, was telling this anecdote to visiting businessmen in the summer of 1993 to illustrate one of the reasons why his country has an unemployment level of 22%, the highest in the European Community.

For the leader of a socialist government to be singling out over-regulated labour markets as a primary cause of unemployment is indicative of a new openness in the EC debate about employment and competitiveness. That openness, driven by new peaks of EC unemployment and renewed worries about competitiveness, was one of the most distinctive and encouraging features of European politics in an otherwise gloomy 1993. It even led the authors of the social chapter of minimum employment rights at the European Commission to tentatively examine whether the high cost and high protection of European workers is one reason why so few of them are employed — 60% of people aged 16 to 64 compared with 75% plus in the US and Japan.

The Commission will, quite rightly, never abandon its commitment to minimum employment rights. And no EC government, let alone the Commission, is seriously suggesting that the EC should try to emulate the US, where two-thirds of employed workers are subject to instant dismissal and far fewer unemployed workers than in Europe qualify for benefit. But in the Commission's Social and Employment Affairs Directorate-General (DGV), and most recently in the Delors White Paper, it has become *de rigueur* to ask whether a more employment-friendly balance can be struck between protecting the securely employed 'insiders' and de-regulating in favour of the unemployed 'outsiders'. As one senior Commission official put it: "We are not saying that de-regulation is the only answer or that everyone should emulate the UK, but some countries do need to loosen up a lot more".

The ratcheting up of EC unemployment since the early 1970s has as many causes as there are countries (and regions) but the hard facts which have prompted the current reassesment are indisputable: the proportion of the working age population in employment in the EC has scarcely risen over the past 20 years and in 1993 nearly half of the 18m EC unemployed had been out of work for more than one year, with 30% having never worked at all. Furthermore, although the rate of growth required to produce net job creation in the EC is now falling towards 2% it has been considerably higher for much of the past 15 years.

**Growth alone is not sufficient**

Indeed, economic growth may be a necessary condition of employment growth but it is evidently not a sufficient one. As Paul Ormerod of the University of Manchester has pointed out, Western economies over the past 20 years have shown enormous diversity in both the rate of job creation and unemployment levels. Between 1970 and 1992, the American economy grew in real terms by 76%, and the EC by 73%. Yet employment in the US rose over the same period by 45%, compared to only 7% in the EC. In most European countries, argues Ormerod, the proceeds of economic growth have been appropriated by those who have remained in employment and the unemployed have been excluded. The Spanish economy illustrates the point: between 1970 and 1992 the economy virtually doubled in size, growing by 93%. But in 1992 employment was actually 2% less than it had been in 1970. Other EC economies show similar patterns. Over the 1970-92 period the total percentage growth in output and employment was, respectively, as follows: Germany 70 and 8; France, 75 and 7; Italy, 84 and 8; and Britain, 52 and 3.

Not everything can be blamed on sclerotic labour markets and some of the jobless statistics are distorted by other factors — in Spain, for example, many people 'sign on' to receive free health care. But even assuming that most EC countries will experience healthier growth following the recasting of the ERM at the end of 1992 it is still the labour markets which will have to adjust if unemployment is to fall back to a respectable level.

Such adjustment is not easy. Labour market regulations, pay-setting systems and welfare regimes, usually have long histories and are not easily disturbed. Moreover, EC job creation in the 1990s faces four additional difficulties. First new technology and competition from low-wage countries, while not a primary cause of unemployment, is phasing out many middle and low skill jobs, from banking to bulk chemicals. Second, big companies seem likely to be net job shedders for the forseeable future. Third, governments facing a fiscal squeeze and seeking to improve the efficiency of their public services are not going to be big job creators, as they have been for much of the 1980s, nor are the utilities which are also striving to become more competitive. Fourth, when the EC created 11.4 million new jobs between 1985 and 1991 only 30% of them went to the registered unemployed because of a growing reserve army of women who come on to the market when jobs are plentiful and disappear when they are scarce. In fact, more than 95% of all new jobs created in the last 10 years have been taken by women.

Mindful of some of these factors, and aware that female participation rates are slowly catching up with levels elsewhere in the industrial world, the Commission estimates that merely to reduce unemployment from 11% to 7% requires the creation of 10 million jobs before the end of the decade. So what medium-term measures should individual countries be considering to create and retain jobs, bearing in mind that none of them have much public money available? And what can EC countries learn from each other's experience?

Debate is now focusing around five main areas of reform: the high costs of firing and the restrictions on part-time and temporary work, especially in the Southern European economies; the relatively high cost of labour and, in particular, the burden of high pay-roll taxes; the low labour-intensity of the service sector; recasting unemployment benefits and active labour market policies, especially education and training, to fit the new realities of atypical work and multi-career working lives; and measures to encourage a more equitable sharing out of the work and incomes available.

The largely political/symbolic argument about the Social Chapter of minimum employment rights in the EC has little direct bearing on these debates. Most EC countries — even the poorest — have employment rights that provide superior protection to the Social Chapter, which is designed to prevent a downward spiral of social dumping. This is, however, less true of Britain which has not had extensive rights at work enshrined in law, one reason for the UK government's hostility to legislation in this field. But behind the political rhetoric it is not simply opt-out Britain versus the rest of high-regulation Europe. For the forseeable future EC social legislation is likely to avoid imposing significant new costs on employers and will concentrate instead on low-cost gestures such as works councils for consulting workers in EC-based multinationals.

Although the UK government exaggerates the extent to which Britain has won the argument on flexibility there has been some shift in a de-regulatory direction, backed by centre-right governments in France and Germany. The labour market reformers in the Commission do not like to use the politically tainted concept of de-regulation but when they talk about solidarity between the employed and the unemployed they are using the language of the left (solidarity) to implement a policy more usually associated with the right (restraining labour costs). They would argue, with some justice, that the coupling together of 'solidarity and competitiveness' is transcending left and right, and that the goal is to make European labour more attractive to employ without reducing levels of protection and increasing social dislocation. The Commission, and most member states, also continue to see an important role for the state and the social partners — unions and employers bodies — in negotiating the necessary changes.

## Hire and fire flexibility

When the aim is to increase employment it may seem perverse to make it easier to fire people. But in increasingly open and competitive markets employers, large and small, will only hire if they know they can fire when market conditions deteriorate. The average cost of firing someone in the EC is 22 weeks pay (26 weeks for white collar workers and 16 for blue collar) and most countries require statutory consultation with unions or the state. Denmark, Ireland and the UK have the least restrictions, Spain, Italy, Greece, Portugal and the Netherlands have the greatest restrictions and Belgium, France and Germany lie in between.

The principle that the more regulation there is to protect standard, full-time, open-ended, jobs, the fewer of them employers will want to offer does seem to be borne out by the Southern European states with their high regulation, low workforce participation rates and high long-term unemployment (with the notable exception of Portugal).[1] Many of these countries have had to absorb large flows of people off the land in the past 15 years but despite fast rates of growth associated with joining the EC none of them has seen a net increase in employment over the last economic cycle.

The legacy of regulation in Southern Europe stems from a time when product markets too were highly regulated, but with the liberalisation of markets the full-time employment guarantee is having to be loosened too. Some countries like Spain and Italy, where it can cost more than two years pay to sack someone from a large company, are in the process of reforming their procedures. There has, indeed, been a slow drift towards de-regulation throughout the EC during the 1980s, a trend which has been reinforced by the election of a centre-right government in France.

There has also been some reform of the tight regulations that the Southern

European countries have inherited on atypical work — part-time and temporary work. In France and Spain, where temporary contract work was liberalised in the 1980s, more than half of the long-term unemployed found employment through such work. In Spain nearly 40% of all employees are now on temporary contracts compared with an EC average of 9%.

Many labour market economists argue that increasing atypical work does not increase employment overall but merely repackages a given number of full-time jobs into a larger number of insecure part-time or temporary ones. This argument still has many supporters in Italy where there is very little part-time or temporary work and private employment agencies like Manpower were banned until 1993, as they still are in Greece.

It may, indeed, be undesirable to allow temporary work to reach the level it has in Spain, where the government is now offering employers subsidies to convert such temporary jobs into normal open-ended contracts. But the evidence from France and the Netherlands shows that part-time and temporary jobs are a useful way for employers to screen employees and often lead to full-time jobs. (One of the biggest obstacles to job creation is the essential decency of many small business people who are reluctant to enter into long-term employment relationships which they fear they will be unable to sustain.)

## Pay and non-wage labour costs

One of the most straightforward reasons for the EC's inferior performance on job creation compared with America and Japan is pay. The pay of EC workers increased at an average of 4% a year during the 1980s while in America and Japan it was virtually static.

It is difficult, in the short term, for governments to have a direct impact on pay-setting except in the public sector or in highly corporatist economies. And linking insider pay restraint to outsider employment opportunities is easier said than done. Padraig Flynn, the EC Social Affairs Commissioner, talks about a "new solidarity" between those with work and those without, but in a decentralised market economy it is a difficult goal to achieve. During the short-lived boom that accompanied German reunification West German workers were asked to show restraint in the name of solidarity with East German workers. But the German unions responded that restraint would simply mean even larger profits for their employers which would be invested abroad and not in East Germany. More recently the French government closely considered a novel scheme to offer subsidies to companies where the workers take a pay cut to preserve jobs, but decided it would be too difficult to police.

Governments can more easily do something about high pay-roll taxes and state wage fixing systems. The Italian government, for example, has recently abolished the *Scala Mobile* which linked pay rises to inflation and the French minimum wage scheme which, according to most studies, has had a negative impact on youth employment, is gradually being reduced. Pay- roll taxes, which add on average 30% to the EC's wage costs, are coming under scrutiny everywhere. In Denmark the pay-roll addition is only 3% and in the UK 13% but in France, Italy and Belgium the average figure is 45% and often much more for higher paid employees.

For historical reasons some countries loaded a large part of the social security burden on employers because there was no other reliable way to collect the revenue. But the burdens on employers are now increasing not diminishing the spread of the informal economy in most EC countries and, according to the OECD, reducing employment, particularly of unskilled, low-wage, workers. Switching the financing of social security away from pay roll taxes could have a positive effect on employment without diminishing security or equity.

Transferring some of these costs to individuals may simply cause wages to be pushed up to compensate and few governments are keen to carry the burden themselves. But the Belgian government is trying to reduce the social security contributions of employers in export industries by introducing a national energy tax and the new French government intends to cut employers contributions to family allowances. Governments with generous unemployment benefits pay a high price for unemployment and it may be cost-effective to shoulder some of employers' non-wage labour costs in order to avoid that unemployment cost.

UK ministers claim that the model for many of these reforms is the low pay- roll tax, easy fire, British labour market. For the low-productivity/low-wage economies of Southern Europe the UK (and US) may, indeed, have lessons to teach. Arguably, the UK has had to have a highly de-regulated labour market because of its historically open and volatile economy — a volatility which has now spread to the Southern European countries. And de-regulation works to off-set many disadvantages such as poor education and training, and low labour mobility, which the UK shares with the Southern countries.

However the British way is less relevant to the high pay/high productivity Northern European countries. In the case of countries like the Netherlands and Germany long-term employer-employee relationships at the workplace and co-ordinated pay bargaining, plus the regulations which accompany them, may have contributed to their high productivity and macro-economic stability. As Ronald Schettkat of the Wissenschaftszentrum in Berlin has pointed out:

> "In a centralized economy committed to wage solidarity, higher wages at the bottom end tend to reduce employment in what would otherwise be low wage industries, while slower wage growth at the top, in what are usually technologically dynamic industries with high productivity growth, reduces relative prices and encourages an expansion of the market and employment growth in these industries. In a decentralized economy, the greater wage flexibility that results allows large numbers of workers to be absorbed into low wage jobs; but the absence of a mechanism for wage restraint in technologically dynamic industries in which productivity is rising may slow the growth of employment at the top".

Indeed, the UK's erratic performance on employment — riding the roller coaster up and then down in the late 1980s and early 1990s — makes it an uninspiring model for the stronger EC economies. The UK has one of the highest employment participation rates in the EC but it also has one of the worst unemployment records, while the three countries with the lowest unemployment rates over recent years — the Netherlands, West Germany and Luxembourg — are all strongly regulated. Over the 15 years to 1992 Germany grew by 2.3% a year and unemployment averaged 6%, while Britain grew by 1.8% and unemployment averaged 9.2%.

And the de-regulated Anglo-Saxon labour markets have come at a price: rising wage inequality and increased social dislocation. Even the creation of 20 million private sector jobs in America over the past 20 years has not solved America's male 'non-employment' problem — 12% of prime age US males — because most of the new service sector jobs have been taken by women. Lower wages for the unskilled have simply encouraged more American men to find alternative sources of income — often selling crack to each other on the streets. Similarly in Britain 14.9% of prime age males were non-employed (unemployed or inactive) throughout the 1980s while both female employment and crime boomed. De-regulation, in other words, may increase labour market participation and female employment but it does not necessarily solve unemployment and carries with it a high social cost.

**Service sector**

But with unemployment now rising fast in most of the more regulated Northern European countries they will not be able to ignore the flexibility agenda. In a modern, competitive, economy exposed to global competition about 10% of all jobs disappear each year. Such a fast pace of change requires rapid changes in the skills and qualifications of the working population, new forms of work organisation, new patterns of working time and new forms of labour contract. Taylorist and Fordist principles of organisation are giving way to a new reality of small units, an overwhelmingly service based economy, a contracting industrial workforce and a need for companies to react to constant market changes.

The service sector is much less labour intensive in the EC than in Japan or America, but also has lower productivity in many key services such as banking, telecommunications and airlines, compared with America. In many EC countries service sector workers with few qualifications are simply paid too much to be worth employing in relation to their productivity. Cutting labour costs in services to individuals not subject to foreign competition directly creates jobs in these sectors. The most socially acceptable way of reducing such labour costs is by reducing social security contributions and other non-wage labour costs for lower paid workers.

The regulatory framework for services also needs review in some countries. Germany, for example, faces persistent structural unemployment, as a result of unification and competitive adjustment in manufacturing. But the service sector is unable to absorb as many of those jobs as it should because of the web of restrictions on things such as Sunday working and shop opening hours. As Gunther Rexrodt, the German Economics Minister, has recently declared, the restrictive practices in the guild-like trade organisations, which, for example, allow a qualified carpenter to build but not to plumb in a sink unit, must go.

Zygmunt Tyszkiewicz, head of UNICE the European employers body, also believes a shift in attitude is required to some kinds of work: "We have cut ourselves off from many of the labour intensive service sector jobs in Europe by importing immigrants to do them. You just have to compare refuse collection in France, where it is a low status job done by immigrants, with Sweden, where it is a dignified and well-paid job".

**Intervening effectively**

The unemployed are not a homogeneous aggregation of suffering humanity. Some of them are high income professionals protected by generous redundancy pay able to step back into employment with ease after a short pause. More than one-third of the EC's unemployed are back at work within four months. But a growing proportion, nearly half, have been unemployed for more than one year, and they tend to be the less well-educated, low skilled, workers whose jobs are disappearing to lower wage parts of the world. For these people there is still an important role for the state through active labour market measures, especially training, and through wage subsidies. According to the OECD, where labour policy activism is higher long-term unemployment tends to be lower.

The EC-funded Ergo programme, which has examined different policy responses to long-term unemployment, concluded that the creation of new enterprises and the encouragement of self-employment was more worthwhile than make-work schemes. Other evidence suggests that public subsidies should be tilted more towards small growing companies rather than start-ups. There is also a strong case for shifting subsidies away from large companies, which in the EC take the lion's share, to concentrate them on small and medium sized businesses.

The Ergo programme also found that counselling measures were the most cost-effective means of getting people back to work. Compulsory interviews and counselling for the long-term unemployed have had positive results in Britain and France, where nearly 30% of those interviewed found either a job or training place. Job clubs, self-help clubs for the unemployed, have also been a successful British innovation now being copied in Portugal.

Counselling is often a way of policing benefit recipients to ensure that they are genuinely seeking employment and is, for that reason, particularly effective in those EC countries where unemployment benefits are open-ended. Open-ended benefits, unless carefully designed, tend to throw up a web of disincentives to return work, especially in low-paid, part-time or temporary jobs, if people lose all their benefit at a stroke.

It has become a commonplace to point out that most of Europe's social security sytems were designed on the assumption of full-time full employment. But it is true that they have failed to adapt to the growth of part-time and atypical employment. The result is that individuals find it difficult to move from unemployment into anything other than full-time work, which is increasingly rarely what is on offer. Part-time employment can leave people with an inadequate wage and an inadequate benefit entitlement. Some people are also put off taking jobs by the high initial cost of leaving benefit and need back to work grants to bridge the gap, as in Japan.

Effective counselling, or any other measure, has its limits when the EC's 18 million unemployed are chasing probably less than 3 million official vacancies. The same is often said of training, but training the unskilled and semi-skilled unemployed for the high-tech jobs of the future, or for self-employment, is not pointless, even when short-term job prospects do not look good. Skilled people can more easily create jobs for themselves and also exert some restraining pressure on the pay of the employed, who know they can be more easily replaced.

The education and training of the employed workforce is also a vital ingredient in competitiveness and, therefore, a preventive measure against unemployment. Relatively high educational standards have been a historical source of strength for the European economies but no EC country has as high a ratio of graduates to population as Japan and the US. The OECD estimates the ratio of entrants to tertiary education to population at 70% in the US and 51% in Japan. EC participation rates vary from 43% in Denmark to 16% in Portugal, with an EC average of 30%.

## Vocational training

Good vocational training for young people and continuing training for the employed is also regarded, throughout the EC, as a necessary condition of economic success. Vocational training tends to be wider and deeper in the more regulated EC labour markets. In Germany only 26% of the working population have no vocational qualifications, compared with 35% in the Netherlands, 53% in France and 64% in Britain. Where there is low regulation, as in the UK, employers have few incentives to train workers in general, transferable, skills, because it is easier to poach. The OECD's latest *Employment Outlook* suggests that the low labour turnover associated with regulated labour markets promotes high training levels while the high turnover of de-regulated markets does the opposite. Also, where there is relatively low dispersion of wages, as in Germany, there are fewer incentives to concentrate training expenditure on the workforce elite.

There are, however, significant differences amongst the more regulated EC economies over the organisation of training and the role of the state. In Germany the system is highly regulated but employer-led, through the local chambers of commerce, and although there is no compulsion to train most larger employers do so with support from the state for the time (one or two days per week) that trainees spend off the job in colleges. In France the state levy system requires companies to spend at least 1.5% of their wage bills on training or pay a similar amount into a national training fund. In Denmark, by contrast, the system is governed by the social partners, and although there is a levy both employers and employees pay into it. In Italy there is also a wage-bill levy on employers but the system is characterised by so much regional variation that one cannot really speak of a national system at all.

In the UK the voluntarist, market-driven training sytem, run by the private-sector dominated Training and Enterprise Councils, has a patchier record than most of the more regulated continental European systems (although participation in vocational training in France is also very low). But partly because initial vocational training in the UK is so weak there is a relatively high participation rate in further vocational training. According to the 1989 European Labour Force Survey about 13% of UK employees were involved in such training at any given time, a figure that was second only to Denmark and well ahead of Germany on 6.3%.

And there are two trends which are likely to make Britain less, rather than more, isolated in the field of training. First, there is a shift towards a more complex mix of private and public initiatives in the training field. Second, as technology becomes more homogeneous, the company-specific training associated with the less regulated labour markets, such as Britain's, is becoming of more general value. Training will remain, for the most part, the responsibility of member states. But the Commission does fund training schemes through the Social Fund and can act as a catalyst for promoting best practice through exchange programmes and EC-wide networks. It can also develop the mutual recognition of qualifications.

Further, although setting targets can sometimes be a futile exercise, the Commission might propose goals for reducing the number of young people who receive no training at all. Alternatively, some training experts have proposed that as part of an attempt to link schools and employers throughout the EC up to 80% of all school leavers and graduates should have access to sandwich courses designed by employers. Although initial vocational training is strongly bound up with national traditions and does not lend itself to European guidance, that is less true of further vocational training. Mr Peter Auer of the Wissenschaftszentrum suggests a Euromodel: "Short-term modules, the certification of which is recognised nationwide, and which can be combined into longer-term and widely accepted qualifications, along Danish lines, are one possible response to the increased requirement for flexibility".

The broader point for public policy makers at a national or European level is that the more incentives there are for people to develop and re-develop their skills as a mobile bread-ticket rather than cling on to particular jobs, the better the labour market should function. This means an emphasis on security of employability, rather than security of employment, and a role for the state in providing a decent welfare net between jobs and possibly a skill voucher system through which the state helps to fund training.

## Sharing out the Work

Public spending on employment adjustment and job-sharing, and other ways of spreading existing jobs and incomes amongst more people, is becoming more relevant as the working life becomes more fragmented.

Whereas 30 years ago most workers might have expected to work for one or possibly two employers for a working life time consisting of 48 hours a week, 48 weeks a year for 48 years, the position is now radically different. People are used to multi-employer working lives and to a much greater range of employment patterns. Reducing the working week has certainly helped to create jobs, especially where pay has been reduced correspondingly. Job sharing could do the same. One proposal is that more people could take one or more years off at certain points in the life-cycle, such as when one's children are young. This pattern of employment is already adopted by many women in Western Europe and, provided a substantial group of men were willing to accept the greater leisure and lower pay which it implies, a large number of jobs could be created.

The UK government abandoned incentives, introduced in the early 1980s, for public sector employees to split jobs. But the Dutch government has recently insisted that all new employees in the public sector are limited to a 32 hour week. And in Belgium it has just been agreed that workers over 55 can work half time receiving a mixture of pay and pension, thereby releasing jobs for the unemployed. The Belgians are also examining incentives for employers to offer career breaks.

The UK government has been quite properly suspicious of short-time working schemes and more general wage subsidies. But the UK ought to re-examine its blanket rejection. Short time working schemes can be a costly way of slowing down necessary restructuring, which is why the UK abandoned them in the early 1980s. But sensitively applied to companies which are experiencing only temporary difficulty they can be a cost-effective way of retaining jobs and skills. Similarly, most studies show that wage subsidies are a relatively inefficient form of job creation, but if they are targeted on the long-term unemployed in the form of vouchers which can be presented to a potential employer they might be made effective. The UK is currently experimenting with such a system and as the country with the highest overtime in the EC it should also examine how to convert some of that overtime into new jobs without upsetting low-paid employees who need the extra money.

Getting Europe back to work requires more than the end of the early 1990s recession. Unless labour markets can become more flexible and state aid better targeted the EC will continue, like many of its members states for the past decade, to produce jobless growth. The signs are that in most EC capitals, and in Brussels, the message is sinking in.

---

[1] This case is powerfully argued by Mr Bill Wells of the UK Department of Employment.

# Chapter Nine

# Beyond the Welfare State

## Frank Field and Jonathan Hoffman

"Thousands of people of all ages were on the streets yesterday demonstrating against the Budget decision on pension payments and contributions announced last week. The deficit of the Social Security Fund has skyrocketed and is now twice the size of the public sector deficit overall. So the Finance Minister has reluctantly decided to phase in a 40% rise in employers' and employees' contributions, together with a phased 10% cut in the real value of benefits. The decision caused uproar — thousands have joined the populist National Front in recent days and the Pensioners' Party is set to pull out of the governing coalition. But the Finance Minister had no alternative. Some of the lenders to the Social Security Fund were threatening to place it in liquidation, and the central bank governor was threatening to resign rather than accede to the Minister's request to cut interest rates to provide cheap finance for the Fund..."

This newspaper report — from London, Paris or most likely Berlin, one weekend in the second decade of the next millenium — is far from impossible. Only this August the German Economics Minister warned that pension contributions would have to rise by "an order of 30% and more" in the next century. Throughout the industrialised world the average age of populations is rising continuously, following a long-established secular decline in the fertility rate.[1] In the European Community the fertility rate peaked at 2.8 in 1965 but by 1980 it had fallen to 1.9 and reached 1.6 by 1990. Together with a rise in the average child-bearing age, this led to a sharp rise in the dependency ratio.[2] In 1980 the dependency ratio was around 22%. On current demographic trends it is set to rise steeply, reaching a peak of 40% by 2040.

Governments have just three choices in order to escape the catastrophic budgetary consequences of this doomsday machine. Two of them — cutting back on benefits and/or raising the retirement age — risk major political backlashes. Only the third — wholesale commitment to private pensions — is a potential vote-winner. The UK, with its long-established mixed system, is the obvious example for other European governments.

Indeed they have no realistic political alternative but to follow the UK lead (of all EC countries only in the Netherlands and Ireland does the incidence of funded pensions even approach that in the UK).

A related question concerns solutions to Europe's unemployment problem. One solution that has been canvassed is more job-sharing and early retirement. In Belgium for example it has recently been agreed that those over 55 can work half time for a mixture of wages and pension, thereby releasing jobs for the unemployed.[3] In France and the Netherlands one-third of men aged 55-59 are now retired, and three-quarters of those aged 60-64. But often the advocates of such an approach fail either to quantify the increased pensions bill, or to identify who will pay it.

State pensions represent Europe's Achilles heel, whereas, paradoxically, private sector pensions (and life assurance, taken out to supplement pensions) could be one of its greatest sources of strength.[4] First, private pensions could promote the flexibility between jobs, regions and countries without which the Single Market will exist in name only. Unfortunately legislation to assure cross-border pension provision in funded schemes is impractical for as long as members of unfunded schemes are tied to their pension provider, and for as long as there are cross-country differences in tax treatment of pension contributions and vesting requirements.

Second, the liberalisation of fund assets allocations would radically improve the distribution of savings, thereby raising growth and generating jobs. At present a significant share of Europe's life assurance and pension fund assets remain trapped within their domestic borders, by prudential rules which are for the most part outdated (and in some cases possibly illegal).

If the Ecu 1500 billion or so in Europe's life assurance and pension funds were so liberated, the stimulus to growth could be considerable. There are two keys which could unlock it. One is a single European currency — whether or not by the Maastricht route. As a result, restrictions on cross-border diversification would become misguided and irrelevant as would preventing an Edinburgh fund manager from investing south of the border.[5] The second is a political agreement to tear down the barriers to diversification.

Although — like motherhood — all European politicians support free capital movements in theory, when it comes to the practice of liberating captive financing, they seem to get cold feet. This is profoundly to be regretted. In our opinion the vulnerability of the single currency key to genuinely free capital movements makes it all the more important to rediscover the other key, which is legislation to tear down the barriers to diversification. The diversification provisions of the Pensions Directive will be a tangible force for growth in future years. It would be a tragedy if — as is threatened — the Directive sinks without trace.

## Pension provisions in Europe — a patchwork quilt

At the target date of 31 December 1992, the crude calculus of legislative proposals showed that the Single European Market was more or less on schedule. Of the key 282 proposals in the Single Market programme, 90% had been adopted. But there remain many areas of national divergence. Amongst the most striking is provision for retirement. Across Europe this resembles a patchwork quilt, with differences *inter alia* in retirement ages; vesting periods; funding arrangements for state schemes (funded versus pay-as-you-go); tax treatment of contributions to private pensions and the income and distribution of those funds; tax incentives for pension provisions to remain within the employer's balance sheet; and — partly in reaction to these other differences — the role of long term savings institutions, life assurance companies and pension funds. To illustrate just this last point, Britain's pension funds account for over one-fifth of household assets, the equivalent of nearly ten times German proportions.[6] In 1990 pension funds held nearly one-third of all UK-quoted securities.

**Pension Funds and Life Assurance Company Assets**

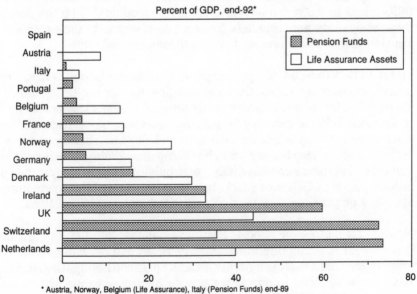

Percent of GDP, end-92*

* Austria, Norway, Belgium (Life Assurance), Italy (Pension Funds) end-89
Belgium (Pension Funds), Italy (Life Assurance), Denmark end-90: Spain, Portugal end-91

As the above chart suggests, the Netherlands, Ireland and Switzerland are the only other European countries where funded pension schemes have developed to anything like this extent. Arrangements in other countries are as follows:—

**France:** Almost all pensions payments are on a pay-as-you-go — or unfunded — basis, administered by *Caisses de Retraite*. The exception is the *fonds salariaux*, which are company schemes, only available to a minority though the original base of top management is now gradually being extended. (Note also that UNEDIC, the unemployment insurance scheme, was FF 24 billion in deficit last year and is losing around FF 1 billion per month.)

**Belgium:** As in France, supplementary pension schemes are increasingly available to white collar workers, on a company basis. However these have to be separately funded where, unlike in Germany, it is illegal to include pension liabilities within the general liabilities of the firm.

**Denmark:** Has started to introduce a supplementary funded pension scheme, which, however, covers less than half the employed workforce.

**Germany:** The State scheme is mandatory and entirely pay-as-you-go. Employee contributions to pension funds are not tax deductible. There is no legal requirement to separate out pension funds and more than 60% of private pension obligations are held within company balance sheets (allocations to the pension reserve are tax-deductible).[7] In a few cases these obligations are separately funded, but this remains the exception. Pension obligations represent 10% of all company liabilities.

**Italy:** In Italy there are few private pension funds, public policy in recent years discouraging rather than encouraging the setting-up of funds, exemplified by an unfavourable tax treatment.[8] Companies are required to set aside 7.5% of earnings for possible severance pay. However, the rules governing payments are such as to make this a valuable source of 'self-invested' cheap finance for Italian companies. Public pensions have been one of the prime causes of Italy's high public sector deficit (estimated around 10.5% of GDP this year). In relation to total public expenditure, spending on pensions rose from 5% in 1960 to nearly 14% by 1990.

**Spain:** As part of the 'Social Pact' negotiations with the unions, the government is attempting to de-index pensions and raise the period of employment required for eligibility. In both Spain and Portugal legislation has been introduced to encourage private funded pensions, but as the above charts suggest, they have not flourished. Some of the reasons include restrictions on where investments can be made, onerous conditions for the granting of tax relief (Spain) and low limits on tax relief (Portugal).

## The future: privatised, portable and funded

Even this brief survey reveals the cross-country diversity of pensions arrangements. But one thing is common to all countries. All governments are trying to extricate themselves from extravagant pensions pledges, made either on a pay-as-you-go or a final salary basis, which are now becoming impossible to fulfil. The most important single cause of this about-turn is demographic trends. But there are two further sources of pressure for greater institutionalised saving — fiscal stringency, and the desire for more responsive labour markets.

## Demographics

The combination of falling birthrates and rising longevity is wreaking havoc with Europe's demographic structure. Overall in the Community, fertility rates peaked in 1965 at 2.8 but by 1980 had fallen to 1.9 and reached 1.6 by 1990 — well below the 2.1 needed to broadly maintain population constant. In 1980 the dependency ratio in the EC was around 22% and will rise steeply to reach 40% by 2040, if current trends are to continue.[9]

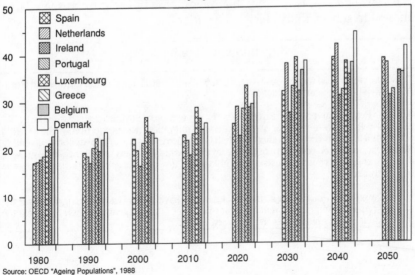

**Dependency Ratios**
Over 65 as a proportion of 15-64

Spain
Netherlands
Ireland
Portugal
Luxembourg
Greece
Belgium
Denmark

Source: OECD "Ageing Populations", 1988

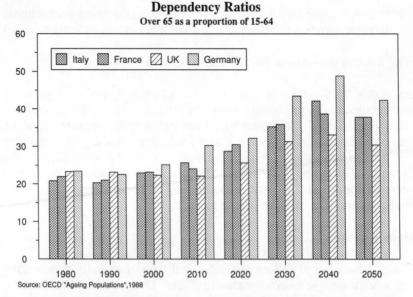

**Dependency Ratios**
Over 65 as a proportion of 15-64

Source: OECD "Ageing Populations",1988

As the above charts demonstrate, nowhere will escape this progressive demographic imbalance. Between 1980 and 2040, the dependency ratio will rise by between one-third and two-thirds in the UK, Belgium and Greece. France, Denmark, Ireland, Luxembourg and Portugal will experience something between a two-thirds rise and a doubling whereas for Germany, Italy, the Netherlands and Spain the ratio will more than double.[10] Neither — as argued in the accompanying box *Migration and Demographics* — is it likely that migration will occur on a scale large enough to substantially change the outlook.

---

**Migration and Demographics**

To what extent could migration — in particular from Central and Eastern Europe and North Africa — alter the demographics?[11]

Not significantly, given the size of the existing population of the European Community (344 million) relative to the size of any conceivable migration (the proportion of the world's population living in a country other than their birthplace is only 1%). The economic incentive for migration may be very high, but as recent elections in Germany and France have proved, there is tremendous political resistance within the EC towards accepting a further large wave of newcomers.

Even if migration remains on a small scale, it may have an impact on demographics if the fertility rate of immigrants is much higher than that of the indigenous population, or if the migration is greatly biased towards the very young.

---

> The first of these possibilities is unlikely:
> - a high fertility rate is arguably the single greatest reason for political resistance to immigration.
>
> - The evidence from most previous waves of migration is that the fertility rate of immigrants tends to fall towards that of the indigenous population.[12]
>
> - In the one case where there could be large-scale migration — of ethnic Germans in the CIS who have the right to settle in Europe — fertility rates are relatively low (2.5 overall in the former USSR, 2.0 in Byelorussia and Ukraine).
>
> What about the second possibility, a migration biased towards the very young? To judge from recent precedents, this too is unlikely. We compared the demographic structure of immigrants into the US, Japan and Germany during the period 1975-1987 with the demographic structure of the population overall (using latest available estimates).[13]
>
> All three countries show an immigrant age structure somewhat different from that of the total population. Compared with the total, fewer immigrants are very old, more are middle-aged, but, crucially, fewer are very young. This type of immigration reduces the current dependency ratio, but — in the absence of higher fertility — raises the future ratio, since the middle age bias will develop into an old age bias in 25-30 years' time, aggravating the bias in the general population.

More elderly in the population means more pension payments and more health care. These trends are already straining public welfare and pension systems. An (admittedly extreme) example is Italy, where pensions spending rose from 5% of total public spending in 1960 to nearly 14% by 1990. The OECD projects that on unchanged policies, the ratio of pensions spending to total public spending will rise to nearly 36% by the year 2040.[14] Much the same trend applies to unfunded salary-related private pension schemes. As far as the problem goes, there is a clear parallel with US healthcare. In the United States companies' health insurance payments — for pensioners as well as current staff — have made serious inroads into their bottom line. Such payments have been rising at a 9-10% rate in recent years; in 1989 they amounted to more than half of pre-tax profits for the entire corporate sector. (A notable example was GM, where equity fell from $30 billion to $6.8 billion in 1992 as a result of the need to meet FASB 106 on accounting for current and future healthcare liabilities: GM pays healthcare insurance for 2 million people, most of whom have never worked for the company.)

In Germany the responsibility of companies to pay salary-related pensions from their own resources will become a drag on profitability in much the same way. German companies will begin to turn to employees for contributions, implying by definition a move to a funded system (by law contributions must be paid into a hypothecated fund). The tendency for medical costs inflation to outstrip the general rate of inflation will exacerbate the problem. But although the problem has parallels with the US healthcare crisis, President Clinton's proposed solution to the latter cannot be a precedent for Europe to tackle its pensions crisis. The Clinton strategy is a two-pronged one. First, the government takes back the responsibility to provide universal healthcare. But as has been argued earlier, European governments, far from assuming additional pension obligations, are trying to divest themselves of the ones they already have. The second element of the US strategy is to increase market pressure on healthcare providers to moderate their prices. This is hardly practical in the pensions area, however.Hagemann and Nicoletti attempt to measure the extent to which public pensions are underfunded. They have calculated the "shortfall" between the present value of pledged pension benefits and the present value of future contributions, taking into account funds already accumulated. The shortfall, shown in the following table, is huge:

| Unfunded Pension Liabilities (% GNP/GDP) | |
| --- | --- |
| US | 158 |
| Japan | 217 |
| Germany | 355 |
| Sweden — non-indexed | 183 |
| — indexed | 228 |

If public sector debt burdens are not to become explosive, there are three possible responses to this shifting demographic balance. First, governments can raise the retirement age. This, however, as we have seen, goes against the grain of creating more jobs. Nevertheless some governments have acted. In Italy in December 1992 the retirement age was raised to 65, from 60 for men and 55 for women. The rise is to be phased over the period to 2002. In the US there will be a phased move (starting in 2003) from 65 to 67, and in Germany (starting in 2001) from 60 to 65. Other Community governments may well follow suit in the light of the Barber Judgement of the European Court (17 May 1990), which decided that, for the purpose of equal pay principal in EC law, pensions should be included in the definition of pay. It therefore required the equalisation of pension benefits — including age of retirement — between the sexes. Given the precarious state of public pension provision, it is hardly conceivable that any government will choose to reduce the age of male retirement towards that of women.

But raising the retirement age courts political opprobrium at a time of mounting disillusion with incumbent governments. The potential for pensions-related pressure groups to gain political office is particularly great in countries with representational electoral systems. For example, the Pensioners' Party in Italy has attracted 9% of the vote in some local elections. In the US a pressure group AIE (Americans for Intergenerational Equity) was set up during the second Reagan administration to call for economic justice for young adults and cuts in social security benefits.

The second possible response is to cut benefits. This is also politically unpopular, but nevertheless several governments have opted for this route. In the UK the first Thatcher government reined back the State provided earnings related pension scheme.[15] Subsequent governments have chosen to uprate pensions in line with prices rather than earnings — as has been recently observed, by the year 2045 this will reduce the value of the pension to a derisory 8% of average earnings.[16] The Netherlands and Sweden have also reduced benefits. In Italy in December 1992 the minimum contribution period was raised from 15 to 20 years. In France the government intends to progressively raise the length of service necessary for a full pension from 37.5 to 40 years as well as increasing the basis of computation from the current 10 years to the average of the best 20 or 25 years. In Belgium an Experts' Commission headed by the central bank Governor Verplaetse recommended (October 1993) raising the retirement age by five years over a 25-year period.

The third alternative is funded pensions. Faced with adequate funding for their retirement, voters across Europe will probably back an increase in savings via pension contributions to funded schemes, rather than an increase in taxation to finance pay-as-you-go provisions. Indeed this would be the appropriate response from the macroeconomic as well as the social standpoint, since it helps to counter the fall in the average savings ratio that will result from an ageing population[17].

In the UK employees have since its inception had the option of contracting out of SERPS, provided they are in an approved alternative private occupational scheme, or of 'subcontracting' their SERPS to a private personal pension provider. In 1988, the government, as an added inducement to contract out, introduced a National Insurance rebate plus an extra two percent "sweetener". As of April 1989, 8.2 million employees were contracted out into occupational schemes, and a further 3.4 million had 'subcontracted' their SERPS to a private provider.[18]

Within the EC, the UK example of a mixed pension system — part funded, part unfunded, part public, part private — stands as an example to the rest of Europe. The UK government's objective should now be to ensure that all citizens gain dual cover of both public and private pensions. The UK pensions model is the one that European governments are beginning to follow. In France, for example, discussion papers on pensions were published in 1991.[19] They projected that contributions to the *Caisse de Retraite* would rise from 19% of earnings to above 30% by the year 2040. They did not recommend a rise in the retirement age but did suggest two alternatives whose effect would be quite pronounced: a lengthening from 37.5 to 42 years of the period of service to qualify for a full pension; and extension of the reference period for pension calculation purposes from the best 10 years to the best 25.

Subsequent to the report the then Finance Minister, Pierre Bérégovoy, announced plans to boost long-term savings, though trade union opposition prevented the introduction of private pension funds. However the current French government intends to introduce pension funds.

In the US, employees without company pensions have since 1974 been able to set up Individual Retirement Accounts (IRAs). These gave full tax deductibility on contributions. In 1981 their availability was extended to all employees, but in 1986 it was again restricted via an upper earnings limit. IRAs have grown rapidly and some $320 billion in IRA money is held in money banks and thrift institutions alone

### Fiscal adjustment

Virtually without exception, governments throughout Europe are trying to reduce their fiscal deficits. The prospect of slow medium term growth exacerbates the problem. Even though there are some doubts whether the Maastricht blueprint for EMU will be implemented, countries are still likely to aim for the Maastricht targets for fiscal convergence. These are a ratio of general government deficit to GDP of below 3%, and a ratio of general government debt to GDP of below 60% (or if greater, "sufficiently diminishing and approaching the reference value at a satisfactory pace"). In 1993 only Luxembourg will meet both these criteria, and the outlook is little different. With demographics working against them, no EC member state can any longer afford to ignore the advantages of moving to universalisation of private pension provision to run alongside the State's own scheme.

A related but separate factor concerns privatisation. Most European governments have initiated some privatisation. (This includes left wing governments — for example the Socialists in France, who sold tranches of Total and Rhône-Poulenc.) However, without a core of domestic institutional investors, privatisation inevitably means raising the extent of foreign ownership of industry, with concomitant political criticism.

## Labour mobility

Fewer than 5% of Europeans work in a country other than that of their birth. Reducing trade barriers will be ineffective as a stimulus to growth if at the same time rigidities discourage workers crossing borders in response to economic incentives. Current pension arrangements, tied as they are to one company (in the form of long vesting arrangements or linking to leaving salary) or to one country (in the form of non-transferability of rights across borders) represent a major such rigidity.

## Diversification: Europe's introverted funds

The 1988 EC Capital Movements Directive was widely seen as successful, leading several countries to remove all controls ahead of schedule. Moreover, despite the ERM crisis which broke in September 1992, Ireland honoured its commitment to abolish controls by the end of the year, and even though the ERM has been forced to move to wide bands and both the UK and Italy to suspend their membership altogether — no-one has wanted to jettison the 1988 Directive.

In view of the primacy clearly attached to free capital flows it is all the more strange that the investment orientation of the prime agents of capital movement — Europe's life assurance and pension funds — is still predominantly introverted.

**Pension Funds**
% Non-Domestic Assets

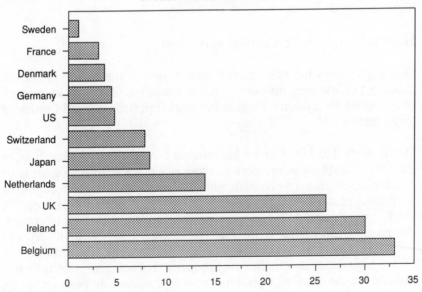

For the international economy to function efficiently it is essential that funds are able to flow from regions of surplus to those in deficit. Imagine the protests from the UK regions if London-based pension funds were only permitted to invest in companies based in the South-East. Yet — as shown in the above chart — that is a microcosm of the position of Europe's life assurance and pension funds. French pension funds are 95% invested at home; Danish funds 99.5%; and Dutch funds 89%.[20]

UK, Irish and Belgian funds have gone furthest down the diversification route. However, even in these countries life assurance and pension funds are well below the level of diversification that might be optimal in a single currency, single market Europe. Take the UK. UK-based Pension Funds have 25% of their investments in non-UK assets. A division of the 25% into Europe and non-Europe is not available but it can safely be assumed that the allocation to Europe is not more than 20%. That contrasts greatly with the weight of the UK in European financial markets. Of EC equity markets, the UK accounts for 44%, so a 'neutral' weight for UK LAPFs would be to have larger investments in EC equities than UK ones. For bonds the 'neutral' weighting should be even more skewed towards the rest of the Community since Britain accounts for only 10% of EC/Ecu bond markets.

Introversion in asset allocation looks even more inappropriate in view of the rise in the proportion of profits earned abroad. In general for the typical European company the non-domestic market accounts for just over half of sales and profits, but for the smaller economies the proportion is much higher.

**Hidden barriers to free capital movement**

One explanation for this striking introversion is the non-uniform tax treatment of investing institutions across countries. But — as in the case of corporate tax systems — growing market pressures should promote convergence.

However the 1988 EC Capital Movements Directive notwithstanding, in the area of institutions investment, there remains a bewildering array of 'hidden' restrictions on diversification. Originally these were imposed for prudential reasons — for example to protect pensioners (Swiss pension funds are forbidden to invest in assets yielding less than 4%), to prevent the erosion of pension rights through exchange losses, or to prevent excessive risk-taking by pension managers. But in view of the commitment to free capital movement, the rising proportion of company profits earned abroad and the Maastricht commitment to a single European currency, many of the restrictions have become simply anachronistic. And those which oblige LAPFs to fund governments are in blatant contradiction to the spirit of Article 104 of the Maastricht Treaty (which prevents governments raiding central banks for finance).

The following are examples of some of the more significant features of this old-style Soviet method of allocating funds. They do not generally include restrictions on asset classes (for example, the requirement for a minimum proportion of assets to be invested in bonds) which are features in a number of countries; nor restrictions on asset mix through discriminatory tax privilege rather than through explicit limits; nor all currency matching requirements.

**Belgium**: *Pension funds* — at least 15% of assets must be held in Belgian government bonds. *Insurance companies* —pension funds with insurance companies must invest at least 15% of reserves in Belgian government bonds. No more than 25% can be invested in foreign equities.

**United Kingdom:** *Pension funds* — no more than half of a fund's assets may be invested in non-EC securities. *Life insurance companies* — there are currency matching requirements, as follows: if a company has more than 5% of its liabilities in a single currency, then the relevant liabilities must be at least 80% matched by assets in the same currency. In other words if (as is a typical minimum) 90% of liabilities are in sterling, then at least 72% of total assets must also be sterling.

**Germany:** *Pension funds and life insurance companies* — rules on foreign investment are highly restrictive. Only 4% of required reserves can be held in non-German equities, and equity investment overall is restricted to 25%. No more than 5% can be held in non-German bonds. Note however that there are no restrictions on investment of assets held in excess of required reserves.

**Greece:** *Pension funds* — virtually all assets are required to be invested in Greek government bonds.

**Netherlands:** *Pension funds* — there are no restrictions on private pension fund diversification. However the civil service pension fund *Algemeen Burgerlijks Pensionenfonds* (ABP, the world's second largest pension fund, with assets of over $90 billion) is restricted both geographically and in the type of securities it can buy: it can invest no more than 5% (zero up to March 1988) abroad, and then only in EC and selected OECD countries; and it can invest no more than 20% of its assets in equities and property. *Life insurance companies* — these are subject both to currency matching rules and rules requiring a certain proportion of assets to be invested at home.

**Denmark**: *Pension funds* — foreign investment is permitted up to 20% of total liabilities. Pension plans with banks must invest 50% in Danish bonds. *Insurance companies* — full currency matching is required.

**France**: *Pension funds* —although regulations on *Organismes de Placement Collectif en Valeur Mobilières* for the most part treat EC and French securities evenly, there are some pension funds where investment in non-French securities is restricted. 34% of the 'stabilisation reserve' of pension schemes must be invested in French government bonds. In addition, for some pension funds tax rules effectively rule out foreign investment. *Life insurance companies* — 100% currency matching of liabilities to assets is required. A minimum of 34% of assets must be invested in public sector bonds.

**Italy:** *Insurance companies*— foreign investment is only permitted to the extent of non-lira liabilities. Even then not more than 20% of technical reserves can be held in equities quoted elsewhere in the EC.

**Ireland**: *Life insurance companies*— no more than 20% of liabilities may be matched by assets in different currencies.

**Portugal**: *Insurance companies*— at least 50% of assets must be invested in Portugal.

**Spain**: *Pension funds and life insurance companies*— both have limits on foreign investment; in addition pension plans may not be sold by institutions domiciled abroad.

### Dismantling the barriers: the prime movers

There are two keys to diversification of assets. One is the market place — provided it is allowed to function, by means of the dismantling of the above restrictions. Capital liberalisation in Europe has made investors increasingly aware of the benefits of portfolio diversification — witness the flood of German investment into the higher yielding bond markets, both after the withholding tax announcement of October 1987 and in anticipation of the imposition of withholding tax at the start of 1992. The second key to diversification would be a move towards a common currency — whether or not via the Maastricht route. This would be bound to hasten the cross-border demand for life assurance and pensions, since at present the vast majority of customers would not dream of buying products denominated in a foreign currency. Contracts will become much more amenable to performance comparison and this will be done more and more, intensifying competition still further. This would in turn raise the pressure for diversification.

But the keepers of the keys — Europe's politicians — seem to have mislaid if not lost them. The always controversial Maastricht timetable for a single currency has been called into question by the currency volatility in Europe over the past eighteen months. And although all European politicians support free capital movements in theory, when it comes to the practice of liberating captive financing, they seem to get cold feet — the Commission's proposals to promote diversification of pension fund assets seem to have run into the sand.

### The pension directive

The Commission's original proposal for a Pensions Directive pressed for full cross-border pensions provision:

> "The possibility to belong to a pension fund established in another member state without legal or financial discrimination is an important freedom and a necessary measure for the completion of the internal market".

However, it soon became clear that this was too ambitious an aim in the short term. As long as members of unfunded schemes were tied to their pension provider, it would be discriminatory to give freedom for members of funded schemes. A second obstacle was the cross-country differences in tax treatment of pension contributions and vesting requirements: in Germany and Luxembourg employees do not have tax relief on contributions; in Belgium fund income is taxed; and in Germany occupational pension funds have a long vesting period, with the qualifying period set by law at 10 years' employment; also workers leaving before the age of 35 generally have no pension entitlement.[21] So the eventual proposals, put forward in 1991 by Commissioner Sir Leon Brittan, stopped short of freeing cross-border membership, although in our view this should remain an important goal.

The Pension Funds Directive was approved by the Commission in October 1991. However two years later it is in severe danger of sinking without trace. As currently drafted it aims to achieve the following liberalisations, in both private and public sector funds:

- Member states will no longer be able to require that a pension fund be locally managed.

- Member states will no longer be able to require a minimum investment in a specified category of asset or a specified location. Maximum limits will still be permitted — presumably because they can be used to promote diversification, though there is clearly a risk that in practice they will take over from minimum limits to hinder diversification (the UK and Ireland are reportedly most concerned about this abuse).[22]

- Member states will no longer be able to require more than 80% of a fund's liabilities to be matched in terms of currency by its assets. For funds whose liabilities are linked to future salaries rather than fixed in monetary terms, the matching requirement may not be more than 60%. Ecu-denominated assets can match any Community currency (an earlier proposal to regard all ERM currencies as matching each other was dropped).

A provision that multinationals will be able to manage their European pension funds on a group basis, with a single fund and manager if they wish, has been dropped. Member States were not generally in favour of this, though businessmen have already expressed regrets at the disappearance.[23]

Why has the Directive run into the sand? In a nutshell, because the stakes are so high. The wave of assaults on the ERM over the past year have made governments acutely aware of the power of financial markets in the absence of formal capital controls. For governments also to relinquish the informal controls is simply too daunting a step to take. Thus only Ireland, the Netherlands and the UK are presently actively supporting the 80%/ 60% rule for currency matching. Others want a more restrictive 80% rule regardless of whether the liabilities are fixed in monetary terms or linked to final salaries. The Dutch authorities are terrified of the large financing hole that would be left in their economy, should ABP be given the freedom to diversify, and argue (contrary to the Commission's opinion) that ABP is a social security body and thus outside the scope of the Directive.

Turning to Life Assurance companies, the Third Life and the Third Non-Life Directives have now been accepted and enter into force in July 1994. As far as cross-border access is concerned, the two Directives are more far-reaching than the Pensions Directive. They adopt the 'passport' system of the Second Banking and Investment Directives, and preclude governments from insisting that a company from another EC state will need to have local establishment in order to operate. As for currency matching, this requirement must by July 1994 be limited to 80% in each currency. Also there is a *de minimis* concession: where currency matching would mean assets in a currency amounting to not more than 7% of the assets in other currencies, the matching requirement can be dropped in the case of that currency.

We believe that the UK mode of pension provision, of a universal state scheme run in harness with funded company or personal pension schemes, is the strongest model on offer in the European Community. The task in the UK now is to universalise private pension provision so that all citizens are owners of two pensions. The challenge to the UK government in Europe is to argue the advantages of their approach so that other EC members' pensions provisions coalesce around the best packages of retirement benefits already on offer in the UK.

In the EC the Pensions Directive must be seen as a means of improving the underlying strength of pension provision throughout the Community, as well as strengthening a unified capital market. After the political fiasco which followed the negotiations on the Maastricht Treaty, further union must be based on responding to practical issues which are either widely agreed in the Community, or can be shown to hold out unmistakable advantages to its voters.

The spread of private sector pension funds throughout Europe as has occurred in the UK, the freedom to provide pensions cross-border and the liberation of asset allocation decisions would have profound benefits for Europe's citizens. The adoption of a UK-type mixed system — part funded, part unfunded, part public, part private — could promote job mobility and radically improve the allocation of savings, thereby raising growth and generating jobs.

There are two routes to this goal — one monetary, the other legislative. The lower the likelihood of a single currency, the more governments should be concentrating on the alternative legislative route. Yet the Pensions Directive has already been watered down. The freedom to provide cross-border pensions was seen as too ambitious at an early stage and the provision for multinationals to manage their European pension funds on a group basis has been dropped. The Pensions Directive's remaining provisions are in real danger of falling victim to narrow national and sectional interests. It would be a tragedy if this were to happen.

---

[1] The average number of live children born to each female. Broably speaking if the fertility rate is steady at 2.1, population will remain constant with a non-skewed age structure.

[2] Defined here as the ratio of those aged over 65 to those in the 15-64 year old age group.

[3] Example quoted by David Goodhart in *European Unemployment*, written for the Prudential Seminar on European Full Employment Policies, September 2-3 1993.

[4] We do not consider in this chapter privatisation of sickness or unemployment insurance. Neither in our view is amenable to wholesale privatisation, since a significant proportion of any population — the old, the chronically sick and the unemployable — will not represent an acceptable risk to a commercial insurer.

[5] The potency of a single currency as a force for growth challenges those who maintain that a single currency is unnecessary for a free trade area (see the speech by the UK Minister for Europe to the European Policy Forum, 7 September 1993).

[6] See E.P. Davis 'The Development of Pension Funds — an International Comparison' in Bank of England *Quarterly Bulletin*, August 1991.

[7] The Fourth EC Directive on Company Accounts (Article 43 (7)) adopted in 1978 suggests that companies identify reserves against social liabilities, including pensions either in their balance sheets or in the notes to accounts — but it is not mandatory.

[8] D. Franco and F. Frasca 'Public Pensions in an Ageing Society — the Case of Italy' in Jorgen Mortensen, ed. *The Future of Pensions in the European Community*, Brussels: Centre for European Policy Studies, 1992.

[9] R. Hagemann and G. Nicoletti *Ageing Populations: Economic Effects and Implications for Public Finance*, OECD Working Paper 61, 1989.

[10] These OECD projections pre-date German unification, but the demographic outlook for united Germany is little different.

[11] Some estimates see migration from East to West Europe of 3 to 4.5 million over the next three years - see *Soviet Emigration: The Impact on Germany*, CSFB Economics, September 1991.

[12] The explanation is partly better availability of contraception, partly because a more urbanised existence, together with greater welfare provision and lower child mortality rates, reduces the incentive for a large family.

[13] For details see J.M. Hoffman *Towards a Single European Capital Market*, Credit Suisse First Boston (1992).

[14] *Ageing Populations: the Social Policy Implications* 1988.

[15] SERPS (State Earnings Related Pensions) were introduced in 1978. However in April 1988 the scheme became less generous, as the government realised that it implied massive future unfunded liabilities. Under the original scheme a pension built up to 25% of the average of the best 20 years revalued earnings. Under the new scheme the pension built up to only 20% of earnings, and those were specified as lifetime revalued earnings.

[16] Frank Field and Matthew Owen *Private Pensions for All: Squaring the Circle*, Fabian Society Discussion Paper No 16, July 1993.

[17] Hagemann and Nicoletti quote a forecast by Heller and Sidgwick that the ageing process could lead to a fall in the G7 savings ratio by between 5 and 15% of GNP.

[18] Those who are not in occupational schemes but who subcontract are counted in the Department of Social Security Statistics as contracted-in.

[19] The Cottave Report and the Brunhes report.

[20] Data reproduced with the permission of INTERSEC Research Corporation.

[21] The relevant law is *Verbesserung der Betrieblichen Altersversorgung*.

[22] If maximum limits were abused, this could be combatted by an infringement procedure which would require a European Court ruling.

[23] The problem of differing tax treatment across countries which could complicate the establishment of pan-European pension funds.

Chapter Ten

# Laying the Foundations
# for the 21st Century:
# a Programme for the Community

John Pinder

## A European perspective

Europe's share of gross world product is over one quarter, but its share of
IT production is only one tenth. This is one of the most striking statistics
in the preceding chapters. At the heart of the current technological
revolution, Europeans have been losing out to the Americans and Japanese.
In line with the problems epitomised in this hard fact, the EC's share of
world export markets has been declining during the past two decades; and
at the same time unemployment in the Community has risen more than in
the United States or Japan. A popular myth would have it that unemployment
is linked with technological success. To the contrary, it is employment that
is linked with a technologically successful dynamic economy.

It follows that a macroeconomic boost to the economy will be short-lived
unless the economy is technologically dynamic. Current euphoria about
a recovery in the British economy misses the point unless it is accompanied
by a determined effort to turn around the long-standing trend of relative
technological failure. While the particular initiatives required for this
must come predominantly from the private sector, public policy also has
an essential part to play in the upgrading of the infrastructure, in terms of
both physical capital and the capacities of the people, or human capital;
and public policy is also responsible for the legal and institutional
framework which should be designed to secure the best use from the
human and physical resources.

Thus macroeconomic policy needs to be accompanied with a programme
for upgrading the human and physical infrastructure and thus for giving
the private sector the confidence required for sustained investment to
make the economy dynamic and create employment. Such a programme
cannot be based on an assumption that the British economy could develop
on more-or-less self-sufficient lines. It has to be seen in the perspective of

an increasingly interdependent Europe which will itself be part of an interdependent wider world. This concluding chapter seeks to draw from the rest of the book some of the main lines that should inform such a European perspective and the ways in which common European action would appear to be indicated.

## Employment policy

Deregulation is the aspect of employment policy that has been most discussed in Britain. Labour markets have been over-regulated, particularly in some of the EC's member states. But that cannot be the whole explanation of Europe's employment difficulties. If it was, highly-regulated Germany and the Netherlands would have more difficulties than Britain, and Japan more than the US. Long-term relationships between firms and their employees, which imply a degree of formal or informal regulation, are a feature of some of the most successful economies. But the structure of labour markets and employment systems varies greatly between different countries and such matters should, as far as possible, be left to the Community's individual states.

The same may be said of pay-roll taxes. In Belgium, France and Italy, where they average 45%, there is more scope for reduction that in Britain, with its 13%, or Denmark, with 3%. The case for the carbon/energy tax, which Belgium and others wish to use to take some of the burden off the pay-roll tax, relates to the environment rather than to employment, even if it could be used more generally to lighten taxation on enterprises. Active labour market policy too, which, as Goodhart points out, is associated with reduction in the levels of long term unemployment, is mainly a matter for the individual states. But it comprises one element, training, which should have a significant European dimension.

Even in Germany, with its strong tradition of training, ground has been lost to Europe's competitors. As Mackintosh notes, Korea has been producing four times as many graduates in IT as Germany (before unification) and Britain together. Upgrading of education and training for technological excellence depends in part on the system of a country: the culture of its enterprises, the public sector, and the interface between the two in taxation and subsidisation. It also depends on the view of the future taken by the people being educated or trained, by their teachers, by business and by government; and if people are to be educated and trained for a technologically dynamic Europe, the perspective of such a Europe has to be apparent to them and the means to take their place in it within their reach.

The Community has done much to ensure the mutual recognition of professional qualifications, so that those who have them can work anywhere among the member states. The standards recognised will have to be continually upgraded to keep ahead of technological developments. Formal qualifications are not enough, however; different languages, cultures and systems are a barrier, which EC programmes such as Erasmus, for student exchanges, Tempus, for cooperation with Central and Eastern Europe, and Lingua for language education in schools do a good deal to overcome. Such programmes should be developed to the point where nobody in the Community is inhibited from exercising the right of free movement because language is a barrier. Nor is the need only for employees to be able to exercise that right. New enterprises, small and medium firms generally, and self-employed make the main contribution to the creation of jobs. Not only should the ability to create jobs in these ways be an important product of education and training, but also should the ability to do so across frontiers, in ways that can make a reality of the Single Market. Employment and enterprise support services as well as education and tradition can contribute to this.

Thus although education and training are largely a matter for the member states, the Community also has its part to play in helping to overcome the barriers to firms and people taking full advantage of the potential of the Single Market; and there must be a high profile for the Community's programme to this end, in order to secure a full enough response from those who should benefit.

**European infrastructure: transport**

In order to compete in world markets as well as to make the most of the Single Market, European enterprises need a well-organised European home base. This is well understood by European business: the European Round Table of industrialists has, as Richardson records, together with UNICE, the European industrial confederation, promoted the idea of a programme to develop the European infrastructure, which received a certain recognition with the concept of the Trans-European Networks introduced in the Maastricht treaty. Transport is one of the fields in which Europe is deficient.

If the Single Market is to work well, it needs an excellent European transport network. The member states tended to establish inward-looking systems, whereas the single market needs inter-operable cross border systems, linking the main centres with each other, and the centre to the periphery. Beyond the EC, it will be necessary to extend such links to Central and Eastern Europe as well as to the world beyond. Yet over the past two decades, transport investment in the Community has declined from 1.5% to 0.9% of GDP. Transport across the borders remains inadequate; and all the member states, not least Britain with its insular and, in part, peripheral position, would benefit from a radical improvement.

Thus it is the common interest to launch a programme to overcome the barrier of inadequate transport. It should be financed mainly by private investment, seeking a good return from the facilities that will get their income from the users. But there will also be a need for a contribution from the public sector. The risk, related to the time scale, may in some cases deter private funds from taking the whole responsibility for investments that will bring a considerable public benefit; and that may be the case when barriers to movement of people and goods across borders are to be moved. the European Investment Bank has much experience of combining private funds with public purposes; and for the relationship with Central and Eastern Europe, the European Bank for Reconstruction and Development is in the process of acquiring it.

If the rate of investment in transport were to return to the former 1.5% of GDP, some Ecu 30 billion of investment funds per annum would be required. The need may well be less than this; and only part would pertain to the European network. But the size of a programme to give Europe the transport infrastructure it needs would certainly be substantial; and it would not only provide an element in the home base that a technologically successful European industry needs, but would also generate considerable employment meanwhile.

**European infrastructure: communication**

Europe needs an infrastructure which enables the use of IT to be a part of everyday life, both in business and in the society. Mackintosh depicts the vision of an electronic communication network across Europe, with a fibre optic, broadband connection to each office, school, hospital, and home. He points out that cable television companies are already making such connections and that here too, Japan and the United States are ahead of Europe.

This, like the transport network, would be a European public good. It would provide both the business communications required by a well-functioning single market and the personal and political connections to give it a basis in the social reality. The construction of this 'neural network', or Eurogrid, would also provide a symbol of Europe's future in a world that will be permeated by IT and would focus the minds of citizens, business and government on preparation to live in that world. As with the transport network, most of the investment could come from the private sector, but the public sector would contribute in order to ensure that the network is complete; and the EC, together with the European Investment Bank, would be responsible for ensuring the completion of the cross-border elements of the network.

Mackintosh cites an estimate of $20 billion (Ecu 17 billion) a year for twenty years to complete the network for the Community. Extensions to Central and Eastern Europe would add to the cost and take longer. If, in the process, the European IT industry could be raised to the level of those in the United States and Japan, so that the Community gained its share of production and employment that would reflect its share in gross world product, the sector would provide over a million jobs, apart from the fallout in other sectors and the jobs created in construction of the network. But Mackintosh points out that the European industry is not at present competitive enough to reap the benefits, most of which would go to American and Japanese companies. There is a small Community preference of 3% for public sector procurement. He suggests that, for a period in which the European industry is being regenerated, more protection than that would be required. But if public intervention if the form of support for the human and physical infrastructure and for research and development can be sufficient, that is clearly greatly preferable, when Europe has a strong general interest in the maintenance of open international markets.

## Environment and energy

A clean environment is a requirement of modern society and business. Cross-border pollution is a clear case of an externality, with people in one country bearing the cost for which those in the neighbouring country are responsible. The Community has enacted over two hundred laws to deal with environmental problems, while the cost of environmental protection has been borne largely by the member states. The Community's programmes of assistance for Central and Eastern Europe have, however, begun to contribute towards the cost of cleaning up the environment mess left by the communist regimes. The full cost of this will be very large, as witness an estimate of some Ecu 100 billion for bringing up to West German standards the environment in the five new Länder alone. If the Community decides that it should do more to regenetrate the eastern economies, in order to ensure their transition to market systems in the framework of pluralist democracies, there would be scope for a major programme of assistance in this field. An important by-product of this could be the strengthening of the Community's industrial base in the field of technology and equipment for environmental protection, which will certainly be a leading sector in the world for a long time to come.

Energy-saving and the conversion to cleaner sources of energy are important elements in environmental protection. Programmes to encourage energy-saving are generally labour-intensive and thus creative of employment. But they are largely within the competence of member states, without any compelling reason to transfer them to the Community level. The proposal for a carbon tax is, however, a Community matter, because of its effects on industrial costs and hence competitiveness; and it deserves a better hearing than the British government has given it so far. In moving towards cleaner sources, Russian natural gas could play an important part. The network for energy distribution is another field in which the European infrastructure needs to be completed; and intensifying the connection with Russia could be politically and economically as well as environmentally important.

**Finance**

With free movement of capital and integration of financial markets, a vast European capital market is in the process of being created, in which institutional investors capable of financing large infrastructure projects are playing an increasingly important part. Bishop cites the estimate of the European Federation for Retirement Provision that the assets of pension funds, currently some Ecu 800 billion, will reach about Ecu 2,300 billion by the end of the decade, thus expanding at a rate of, say, Ecu 200 billion a year. Life assurance institutions, at present with larger assets than the pension funds, have also been expanding; and enterprises such as the mutual funds too have to be taken into account. Infrastructure programmes on the scale mentioned above can be accommodated by institutions receiving such funds.

Behind the growth of pension funds is a daunting problem of the age structure of Community citizens. The reproduction rate in the EC is now 1.6, which implies a formidable growth in the proportion of national income that will be required to maintain a decent living standard for pensioners: as far as the pay-as-you-go public sector schemes are concerned, this is a doomsday machine, in the words of Field and Hoffman. If these schemes were to continue to bear the predominant share of the burden that they do in most member states, either the working population will have to pay sharply higher taxes, or the pensioners' incomes will have to be severely cut. The radical tax rises and benefit cuts that would be required to balance the books are hardly practicable in democratic countries: hence the attraction of an expansion of private funded schemes, in which people save during their working lives to acquire assets that will bear the income for a decent pension when they retire. Britain, Ireland and the Netherlands are the only member states in which such schemes already play a large part. But the others are, as Field and Hoffman put it, "racing to catch up." This means that, at least for the next twenty or thirty years, there is likely to be a heavy flow of savings into pension funds which will need safe yet profitable investments in order to be able to pay the pensions their customers will expect.

The private schemes are not likely to replace the state schemes, but to supplement them, thus providing another example of the symbiosis of private and public sectors in the modern economy, in this case of private and funded with public and unfunded schemes. The private schemes will be subject to regulation to ensure prudent management of their funds; and this will make the infrastructure programmes described above, with their mix of private capital and public support, attractive investments for them. It is fortunate that the prospect of large amounts of money seeking safe investments should coincide with a need for just such money to create the infrastructure for a dynamic European economy. It is not only the safety of these investments that is appropriate for their investment funds and life assurance institutions, but also their contribution to a dynamic economy, without which the funds and institutions will not be able to provide over the long term the incomes that their customers want.

The EC has enacted much of the legislation to ensure the integration of financial markets, including the third Non-Life Insurance Directive and the third Life-Insurance Directive, which give the insurance companies a 'passport' to conduct their operations throughout the Community as from 1 July 1994. But the Pension Funds Directive remains stuck in the Council of ministers. This Directive would not only offer a better deal to pensioners, whose money could be more profitably invested, but also improve the allocation of labour and of capital in the Community, by breaking the restrictions that existing legislation imposes on the investment of pension rights from one country to another. It would also enable citizens to choose a pension fund managed in another member state should they wish. But member states are evidently worried about the necessary changes in the arrangements for taxing pension contributions and their regulations for membership of pension schemes. Unless the Directive is approved, Europe will forgo not only a benefit for its citizens who are saving for their old age, but also a more general economic benefit, in particular in the completion of the European capital market which should make the infrastructure programmes possible at a reasonable cost.

It should be added that the single currency will remove many of the problems with which pension funds and those who invest their assets have to grapple.

## Monetary integration and macroeconomic policy

The project for economic and monetary union, with single currency and European Central bank, would ensure the existence of the European capital market with enough money available on the best terms for programmes of investment such as a dynamic European economy will require. It can also offer the best prospects for monetary stability; and it is a sad reflection on Britain's devaluation culture that so many politicians and commentators have been so eager to write EMU off as a result of the monetary difficulties of the recent period. But the single currency is still likely to be realised. The recent troubles have been due largely to the aftermath of German unification. These effects will diminish in the coming period; and there is no reason to believe that the French government will abandon this central element in its European policy, or that the German government will renege on its treaty obligations with respect to EMU, once the exceptional strains that followed German unification have eased. Both France and Germany have benefited too much from integration in the Community to wish to abandon the project now.

Meanwhile, the European Monetary Institute is being put in place and will seek to further monetary stability in the Community. It would do well to consider the concept of a target for nominal GDP, advocated consistently by Samuel Brittan in the *Financial Times*. But policies to suppress inflation will still have to contend with the endemic tendency towards cost push in our economies, due not just to trade union organisations but to the structure of interdependence in the modern economy, which gives bargaining power to countless individuals and groups who can disrupt the production process by withholding their labour. Germany and Japan have had some success in dealing with this through strong collective control over the individual, by German trade unions and Japanese enterprises and enterprise unions. But this success is only limited. The promotion of competition in the labour markets is the other main method. But given the imperfections inherent in the markets, against which macroeconomic policy has to contend in its attempts to counter inflation, cost push remains too strong unless unemployment is painfully high. No satisfactory solution to the problem has been found so far. But there are ways in which it can be alleviated; and one of these is to increase competition in both product and labour markets by extending the area of free movement of goods and people, as is the aim of the single market project. The greater the success in making a reality of the wider market, the more of the strain of countering inflation can be taken by competition and the less need for deflationary macroeconomic policies; and the same may be said of the upgrading of human and physical capital, in so far as it enables productivity to grow faster and thus accommodate the desire for rising real incomes.

## The international economy

Interdependence is already intense among the member states of the EC, which do over half their trade with each other. But it is also a growing fact of life in the wider international economy. Europeans will not be successful if they try to go against the grain of this international interdependence, which has its roots in the need for a wide market to tap the potential of scale, specialisation and competition. This is why a positive result for the Uruguay round is so important.

Since the Uruguay round has not been concluded while this is being written, space is not given to discussing its consequences. Clearly, if it fails, there will be great difficulty in keeping open markets in many parts of the world. But given that it succeeds, it will be necessary to look ahead towards the next stage in the development of the international economy. This will involve strengthening the international institutions and giving them some of the functions in opening markets that the Community has pioneered with the Single Market project. One element, as Wilkinson points out, will be the establishment of a competition policy, designed to ensure that the big companies which have come to dominate many sectors of the world market do not distort or stifle competition.

Once established in a market, the big companies cannot be expected to remain job creators for long; and this is just as well, because if they continued to swell the numbers they employ, they would become yet more dominant and would, moreover, probably decline in efficiency. Their value to the economy is in a different dimension. They embody the interdependence that is an essential feature of the modern economy. More than other firms, they transmit technology, management, marketing and financial skills across frontiers and continents. Thus the Americans and Japanese are among the best placed to realise the potential of the single market.

Transnational companies tend, as Hu points out, to keep the best work — higher management, research, and technological development — at home or in the hands of their own nationals. Thus while it may be possible to persuade them that it is in their own interests to upgrade the skills of their employees in the countries where they invest, they should not be expected to be the main generators of upgrading and growth. For this, more can be expected of the transnational companies that originate in the Community.

The European transnationals tend to be more integrated into the European partner countries than do the Americans or Japanese. Thus the companies originating in Britain, Belgium and the Netherlands do about half their research and development in other countries. Bishop predicts, moreover, that the financial institutions which will channel more and more of the people's savings into the European capital market will become the most important owners of these companies. They should use their influence to ensure that the European transnationals become more genuinely European, because that will enable these companies to reflect better the interdependent economies and thus to perform better in them. Such companies should also act as transmitters of factors that bring success in other continents where they operate, such as the Asia-Pacific region. Nearer home, the European transnationals have, as Richardson observed, been among the strongest advocates of the infrastructure developments needed to provide a sound home base for European industry, including, of course, themselves. In short, these companies are a valuable European asset and should receive due encouragement from the Community as well as from the member states in which they originate.

## Driving forces and politics

The policies and programmes suggested in this chapter are intended to go with the grain of the driving forces mentioned by Cowie in chapter one. Interdependence is reflected in the whole. The programmes for upgrading the human and physical infrastructure are designed to accommodate the technological driving force. Financial integration is the force behind the proposals for currency integration and capital markets, together with another driving force in the form of the demographic trend towards an older population. The growing post-materialist influence is reflected in the suggestions regarding the environment and— a subject about to be broached—the democratic development of the European Parliament.

Unfortunately political forces often stand in the way of the driving forces, making it harder for the societies they influence to come to terms with the realities with which people have to live. This has too frequently been the case with respect to British governments and their resistance to the implications of interdependence as reflected in the development of the Community. The Single Market programme, strongly supported by Britain, was a notable exception, but British policy at present seems set to oppose the strengthening of the Community's institutions, which growing Community responsibilities and its forthcoming enlargements are likely to demand. Majority voting in the Council is one example of necessary strengthening. It is simply not practical to expect the Community to function under a unanimity rule as it is enlarged from twelve to, say, fifteen, then twenty, then twenty five and more. Nor is it compatible with democratic principles to deny legislative powers to the European Parliament, on an equal basis with the Council, when member states' parliaments have lost the control that they could, at least in theory, exert over the Council when their ministers could veto decisions there. Yet the British government appears unwilling to contemplate the Community becoming more efficient and democratic in these ways. It may be hard for business people to regard Community programmes to deal with the technological and other driving forces as credible if governments refuse the adjustments to institutions that would enable the Community to handle these tasks.

## British interests

The proposals for Community policies and programmes, focusing on human capital and an infrastructure investment financed by pension funds and other institutions associated with the growing savings of an ageing popultation, meet British interests in a number of specific ways. Thus the development of transport and communication infrastructures would help to counter the geographical disadvantages, particularly of our more peripheral regions; and they would also help to remedy some of the defects in our existing infrastructures. The liberalisation of pension fund operations would give the managers of British pension funds the chance to use their skills across the wide Community market; and it would also correct the unfair bias in capital markets and balance of payments due to the fact that British pension funds can and do invest a quarter of their assets abroad while the proportions in France and Germany are of the order of 4-5%. The reasonable mix of private and public elements in the programmes proposed might help British politics to break away from the outdated quarrel between individualist and collectivist ideologies which still damages the process of government in this country. Most important, perhaps, successful programmes on the lines proposed could help Britain to break out of its inhibiting conjunctural cycle.

More generally, a healthy European economy is necessary for Britain since so much of the British economy depends on relations with our European partners; and successful programmes would help to create such an economy. Full British participation in such a major operation would, moreover, place Britain at the heart of Europe, where British political skills could be used for mutual benefit instead of, as so often in the past, being relegated to the sidelines because Britain is perceived to be blocking rather than furthering the Community's development. The history of the Community, from customs union to the single market, has shown that such enterprises are a positive sum gain: the sum gained in value added is large and all can have a share in it. All, and most of all the British, will benefit if Britain plays a full part in launching this new enterprise and participates wholeheartedly in its development.